W9-CUE-040

TOYS

FROM CONCEPT TO CONSUMER

BY KEVIN CUNNINGHAM

CHILDREN'S PRESS®

An Imprint of Scholastic Inc.
New York   Toronto   London   Auckland   Sydney
Mexico City   New Delhi   Hong Kong
Danbury, Connecticut

CONTENT CONSULTANT
Nate Lau, Toy Designer, Tegu

PHOTOGRAPHS © 2014: Alamy Images: 15 top (Chris Willson), 24 left (Design Pics Inc.),
53 (DWImages), 7 (Finnbarr Webster), 17 (Gunter Nezhoda), 10 (H. Mark Weidman
Photography), 54 bottom (Image Source), 14 right (INTERFOTO), 41 left (Jeff Greenberg
"0 people images"), 15 bottom (Paul Carter), 12 top (Robin Beckham/BEEPstock), 13,
29 bottom (ZUMA Press, Inc.); AP Images: 12 bottom (Cheryl Gerber for Mattel), 50 (Court
Mast/Yahoo!), 2 (Craig Ruttle), 34 (Gene Kaiser/South Bend Tribune), 16 left (Jason
DeCrow/Invision for Hasbro), 27, 61 (Mark Lennihan), 9 (Matt Rourke), 39 (Michael
S. Wirtz/The Philadelphia Inquirer), 59 (Press Association), 28 top, 29 top, 4 right, 26
(PRNewsFoto/Activision Publishing, Inc.), 23, 58 (Rex Features), 44 (Sebastian Widmann/
dapd), 46 (SIMON ISABELLE/SIPA), 51 (Sipa); Corbis Images/Lego: 14 left; Dr. Barry
Kudrowitz: 48, 49 top, 49 bottom; Dreamstime/Rigmanyi: 55 left; Getty Images/Dorling
Kindersley : 4 left, 8; iStockphoto/Tom Brown: 28 bottom; Media Bakery: 20, 24 right, 25
top, 38, 54 top; Courtesy of Nate Lau: 36 bottom, 36 top, 37, 55 right; Nathan Sawaya,
Inc./www.brickartist.com: cover, 3; Newscom: 19 (CB2/ZOB/WENN), 42 (David Toerge/
BlackStar Photos), 30 (KENNELL KRISTA/SIPA), 57 (Lu Hanxin/Xinhua/Photoshot), 22 (MBR
KRT), 31 (Ross Hailey/MCT), 16 right (Splash News); PhotoEdit: 40 (Annette Udvardi), 18
(Cindy Charles), 5 right, 47 (David Young-Wolff), 5 left, 41 right (Michelle D. Bridwell), 25
bottom (Richard Hutchings); Superstock, Inc.: 52 (Asia Images), 6 (DeAgostini); Thinkstock/
iStockphoto: 56; Zuma Press/Tan Jin/Xinhua: 35.

LIBRARY OF CONGRESS CATALOGING-IN-PUBLICATION DATA
Toys : from concept to consumer / by Kevin Cunningham.
    pages cm. — (Calling all innovators, a career for you)
Audience: 9–12.
Audience: Grade 4 to 6.
Includes bibliographical references and index.
ISBN 978-0-531-26522-2 (lib. bdg.) — ISBN 978-0-531-22010-8 (pbk.)
1. Toys—Design and construction—History—Juvenile literature. I. Title.
TS2301.T7C754 2013
688.7'2—dc23   2012034207

All rights reserved. Published in 2014 by Children's Press, an imprint of Scholastic Inc.
Printed in the United States of America 113

1 2 3 4 5 6 7 8 9 10 R 23 22 21 20 19 18 17 16 15 14

science, technology, engineering, arts, and math are the fields that drive innovation. Whether they are finding ways to make our lives easier or developing the latest entertainment, the people who work in these fields are changing the world for the better. Do you have what it takes to join the ranks of today's greatest innovators? Read on to discover whether toy design is a career for you.

TABLE *of* CONTENTS

In the past, wooden dolls and other toys were often homemade.

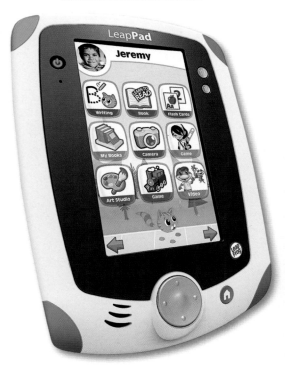

LeapPad is a top-selling toy because it offers kids a variety of fun and educational activities.

When it comes to selling big in the toy industry, a toy's packaging is almost as important as the toy itself.

AN INTERVIEW WITH

Toy Designer Nate Lau

A prototype is one of the first steps in the production of a toy.

This toy was discovered in the ancient ruins of Mohenjo-daro, in what is now Pakistan.

PLAYING IN THE PAST

From kids spending entire afternoons building cities out of colored blocks, to adults collecting their favorite action figures and competing at board games, almost everyone enjoys toys. Whether you're into the robots, video games, and other technological marvels that are all around today, or your toy box is filled with more traditional action figures, dolls, **die-cast** cars, and blocks, you have probably enjoyed countless hours of fun playing with your favorite toys.

People have been making and playing with toys for thousands of years. The ancient Greeks made dolls, while the ancient Chinese are famous for their beautiful kites and wooden puzzle toys. The wheeled, animal-shaped toys of Central America's ancient Olmec people are not all that different from today's toy cars and trucks. Just as they do today, toys kept kids busy in ancient civilizations while teaching them important life skills and encouraging creativity.

20TH-CENTURY TRIUMPHS

1902	1949	1952	1964
The first teddy bears are sold.	The first Lego bricks are released.	Mr. Potato Head becomes one of the most popular vinyl plastic toys.	Mattel releases G.I. Joe, the first action figure.

INDUSTRIAL INNOVATIONS

Toys have existed since ancient times, but kids in the past did not always have as much time to play as they often do now. Instead, they had many household chores and often worked jobs to help support their families. In colonial America, many children did not even have time for school. Instead, they learned valuable skills during the small amounts of free time they had playing with homemade toys. Wooden animal figures helped teach about farming, while simple rag dolls gave young girls practice in raising children. Other popular toys of the time included spinning tops, wooden soldiers, whistles, and drums.

In the early 1800s, people began to buy factory-made toys and gradually stopped making their own. Factories could easily make metal toys, which soon became more popular than wooden ones. Metal roller skates were a hit in the late 1800s. Tin soldiers and animals were also popular.

PAPIER-MÂCHÉ HEAD

HANDMADE CLOTHING

WOODEN LEGS

PAINTED SHOES

Dolls were once made mainly of wood and dressed in handmade clothing.

While today's crayons come in dozens of colors, early Crayola crayons offered only eight color choices.

LARGER BOX →

BUILT-IN SHARPENER →

TOYS OF THE TIMES

The toy business was interrupted when the U.S. government needed metal, rubber, and other materials to make supplies for troops during the Civil War (1861–1865). After the war, new toys reflected a widespread fascination with machines. Iron train models became popular as real-life railroads sprang up across the nation, and the invention of the automobile and the airplane made toy cars and planes a must-have gift.

But two of the most iconic toys of the following decades had nothing to do with machines. In 1902, a newspaper cartoon about new president Theodore "Teddy" Roosevelt inspired Brooklyn shop owners Morris and Rose Michtom to make and sell a stuffed bear. Their teddy bear, named after the president, became an instant best seller. Soon, dozens of companies jumped into the teddy bear business. Bears from Winnie the Pooh to Paddington have stayed on toy shelves ever since. Another toy legend got its start the next year, when Crayola's original box of eight colored crayons arrived in stores. Though crayons had existed in some form for hundreds of years, it was Crayola that brought them true popularity as art toys.

FIRST THINGS FIRST

TECHNICIAN

CONTROL PANEL

COMPLETED PIECES

Plastic molds made it easier for toy makers to create large numbers of identical toys.

PLASTIC'S PROGRESS

It's hard to imagine a time when most toys and other household items were made out of metal or wood. Today, it is far more common for such things to be made from plastic. Plastic is an inexpensive substance that can easily be **molded** into almost any shape. Its rise in popularity during the 20th century made it an important part of many of the world's most popular toys.

EARLY RESISTANCE

The first widely used plastic, **celluloid**, appeared in 1869. Unfortunately, celluloid easily caught on fire—a major safety hazard. In addition, this plastic seemed cheap and flimsy compared to wood or metal. It took sturdier kinds of plastics, lower prices, and good advertising to convince consumers that plastic toys were a good idea.

George Lerner's Mr. Potato Head doll became one of the most popular vinyl toys when it hit stores in 1952. Children built the potato-shaped character's face using a variety of removable plastic eyes, ears, and other features.

SHAPES AND SIZES

In 1872, the brothers John and Isaiah Hyatt put plastic to use with a process called injection molding. In injection molding, tiny pieces of plastic pass through a tube. Inside the tube, heat softens the raw plastic. The machine then presses the melted plastic goo into a specially shaped mold to form buttons, combs, or other items.

SAFETY FIRST

A safer, tougher plastic called **vinyl** replaced celluloid in most products by the 1950s, bringing a new generation of toys. ✺

Later versions of Mr. Potato Head took advantage of new types of plastic.

ALL DOLLED UP

With the rise of plastic, by the mid-20th century toy inventors were free to let their imaginations run wild. A variety of plastic dolls shaped like babies and young girls were among the best-selling toys of the time. Many of the dolls had special features to help set them apart from competitors. Mattel's Chatty Cathy doll had a small record player inside her. Pull a string, and she said one of 11 phrases on the record. Other popular dolls cried or wet their diapers like real babies.

In 1959, Mattel released a new doll named Barbie. Unlike most other dolls of the time, she had the body of an adult woman instead of a baby. Barbie was an immediate hit. Mattel quickly began releasing a variety of Barbie products, including outfits, cars, and a boyfriend named Ken.

The original Barbie doll is not much different from the ones sold today.

RUTH HANDLER

Barbie was created by Ruth Handler, who cofounded Mattel along with her husband. When Handler first pitched the doll to her husband and the rest of Mattel's executive board, her idea was rejected. Handler persisted and eventually convinced them to produce the doll. Barbie became one of the most popular toys of all time, and Handler went on to become Mattel's president.

Ultimate Frisbee is a popular game in which teams compete to score points by passing a Frisbee across a field to an end zone.

ON THE FIELD

Newer types of plastic were not only easy to mold but also durable and easy to clean. This made them perfect for a variety of inventive new outdoor toys. David Mullany invented the Wiffle ball, a lightweight, plastic baseball substitute, in 1953. The lighter ball allowed Mullany's young son to practice throwing curveballs and other tricky pitches without tiring his arm.

On Thanksgiving 1937, Walter Morrison discovered that disc-shaped cake pans made excellent flying toys. He and his wife began selling the pans as toys at local parks. After serving in World War II (1939–1945) as a pilot, Morrison returned home and developed a molded plastic version of the discs, which he called Pluto Platters. In 1957, he sold the invention to the Wham-O toy company, who marketed it as the Frisbee.

In the early 1960s, chemist Norm Stingley discovered that a certain kind of rubber could be used to create incredibly bouncy balls. Stingley sold his invention to Wham-O, who marketed it as the Super Ball. When the Super Ball hit stores in 1965, it became an instant sensation and remained a best seller for years.

PAST MARVELS

This man is working at the original Lego workshop in the Danish city of Billund.

THE PERFECT DESIGN

Each Lego block has pegs on top and holes on the bottom so they can lock together. After the introduction of the first Lego bricks, the company slowly refined the design until it was perfected in the late 1950s. Since then, all Lego bricks have been created using the same measurements, which are planned down to the **micrometer**. This means that Lego pieces purchased today can connect just as well to Legos from 1960 as they can to modern ones!

Early Lego pieces came in a smaller range of shapes than today's pieces do.

THE LEGO LEGACY

Not all toys need modern technology or flashy new features to stay popular. Some toys are such good ideas that they remain popular for decades. In 1932, Danish carpenter Ole Kirk Christiansen founded a toy company and named it Lego, from the Danish words for "play well." At first, the company focused on wooden toys, but in 1947 it began experimenting with the new possibilities of plastic. Two years later, the first studded, interlocking Lego bricks were sold.

On average, people around the world purchase about seven Lego sets per second.

BUILDING NEW WORLDS

The 1970s saw the introduction of the first Lego "minifigures," which are small plastic characters that can interlock with Lego pieces. In the following years, Lego began to introduce a variety of themed sets, allowing kids to build models such as castles, spaceships, and trains.

Around 19 billion new Lego pieces are created each year.

NEW WAYS TO PLAY

In 1969, Lego began selling a new system of building toys that it called Duplo. Duplo pieces are much larger than regular Lego pieces, making them a better choice for small children who might swallow small items. As these children got older, they could use the smaller Lego bricks along with their Duplo pieces. This ensured that kids would not outgrow their old Lego toys.

In 1977, Lego released the first sets in its Technic system. Like Duplo pieces, Technic sets could be combined with standard Lego pieces. However, they were aimed at older children who might want to build realistic vehicles with small moving parts. ✳

READY FOR ACTION

Toy companies began selling sets of green plastic army men after World War II. They quickly became popular among young boys. War toys became even more popular in 1964, when Hasbro released G.I. Joe. The original G.I. Joe was very similar to a Barbie doll. It was about 12 inches (30 centimeters) tall and could be outfitted with removable uniforms and accessories. The creators at Hasbro did not think boys would want to play with something called a doll, so they called G.I. Joe an "action figure." It was the first of its kind.

In the following years, toy companies began making smaller action figures made entirely of plastic, with no removable clothing. These figures became a sensation in 1977, when Kenner released a series of toys based on the movie *Star Wars*. Doll-like action figures were no longer popular, and Hasbro soon redesigned G.I. Joe to be more like the *Star Wars* toys.

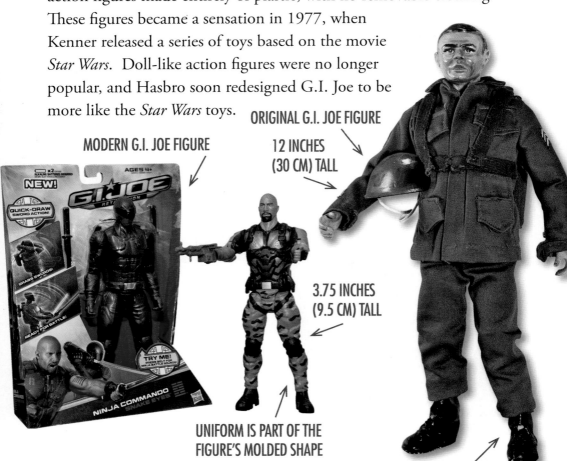

MODERN G.I. JOE FIGURE

ORIGINAL G.I. JOE FIGURE

12 INCHES (30 CM) TALL

3.75 INCHES (9.5 CM) TALL

UNIFORM IS PART OF THE FIGURE'S MOLDED SHAPE

CHANGEABLE UNIFORM

ROAD WARRIORS

Young kids have long been fascinated with cars and trucks. In the 1950s, the British company Lesney Products began to sell small die-cast metal vehicles. The toys were known as Matchbox cars because their packaging looked like the boxes that matches came in.

In the late 1940s and early 1950s, Mound Metalcraft of Minnesota manufactured a variety of household metal goods. But the business really took off in the mid-1950s when it changed its name to Tonka Toys and began producing die-cast toys. The company's sturdy yellow dump trucks and other construction vehicles became its most famous products.

Mattel launched its Hot Wheels line in 1968. Fake rubber wheels made the toys roll faster than any other die-cast vehicles. Hot Wheels also came with eye-catching paint jobs and crazy features such as oversized engines.

Die-cast toys, such as this Matchbox car, are made of durable molded metal.

More than 4 billion Hot Wheels cars have been produced since 1968.

Ty Inc. created more than 1,700 different Beanie Babies.

FUZZY FRIENDS

Always popular, huggable plush toys became bigger than ever in the 1980s and 1990s. Xavier Roberts, a college student, designed the large-headed Cabbage Patch Kids in 1978. The plush dolls reached stores four years later and began selling at an incredible rate. Roberts's creations were so popular that parents were forced to search frantically through sold-out stores to find the dolls at Christmastime.

Former plush toy salesman Ty Warner launched the Beanie Babies in 1993. Each "Beanie" was part plush toy and part beanbag. Warner's company, Ty Inc., steadily introduced new Beanies while retiring older models. This created a demand among collectors, as people combed toy store shelves for rare and valuable Beanies.

Tickle Me Elmo, a talking plush doll based on the popular Sesame Street character Elmo, was in such high demand near Christmas of 1996 that shoppers sometimes fought each other while trying to purchase it!

AMAZING ART TOOLS

Art toys have gone through many changes since the crayons and finger paint that were popular in the early 1900s. In the 1950s, French electrician André Cassagnes combined glass and aluminum powder to create a new kind of drawing toy. Users could twist knobs to etch a design in the aluminum powder behind the glass, then shake it up to erase their drawings and start over. Cassagnes called it Telecran, but it became famous when the Ohio Art Company released it as the Etch-A-Sketch.

André Cassagnes originally named his invention L'Ecran Magique, or "The Magic Screen."

In the 1960s, British **engineer** Denys Fisher used one toy to create another when he built the Spirograph from Meccano building kits. Using a Spirograph, artists can easily draw a variety of highly complex curved designs.

Hasbro's Lite-Brite, introduced in 1967, allowed children to create pictures by placing colored plastic pegs into a light box. When the box was turned on, a lightbulb inside caused the colored pegs to shine brightly.

In 2010, an official Lite-Brite app was released for the iPhone and iPad, allowing users to create classic Lite-Brite designs using their touch screens.

Many of today's toys are built using the latest robotics and computer technology.

2

TODAY'S TOP TOYS

Some things never change. Kids today still play with dolls, yo-yos, blocks, and countless other toys that are popular even decades after they were introduced. At the same time, toy designers are always hard at work looking for new ways to have fun. They might invent something new simply by tweaking an old classic. Other times, a toy designer will come up with an idea so fresh that no one could have predicted it.

Today's most popular toys allow kids to explore virtual worlds and take advantage of the latest technology. The lines between computers and toys are starting to blur as designers search for new ways to make their products more interactive.

HIGH TECH TOYS

2009	2009	2011	2012
Robotic Zhu Zhu Pets become one of the latest "smart toys" to catch on with kids.	Lego releases Mindstorms NXT 2.0, its latest robotic building system.	Skylanders lets video game players bring their action figures into a virtual world.	Mattel's Apptivity toys let kids use special action figures and toy cars to play games on iPad tablets.

GET SMART

Have you ever wanted your own robot? In the 1970s, the invention of inexpensive **microprocessors** opened the door for robotic "smart toys." A smart toy is equipped with electronics that allow it to respond to its environment. Some smart toys can learn basic tasks and interact with their owners through voice and facial expressions.

Earlier smart toys, such as 1985's Teddy Ruxpin and 1998's Furby, could speak and move their faces, but not do much else. Today's smart toys are much more advanced. In 2005, the WowWee toy company released a small robot called RoboSapien. Designed by physicist Mark Tilden, the robot can be programmed to walk, talk, and even pick up and throw small objects.

In 2009, Russ Hornsby's Zhu Zhu Pets became one of the latest smart toy crazes. These small plush hamsters walk around and act like real pet hamsters.

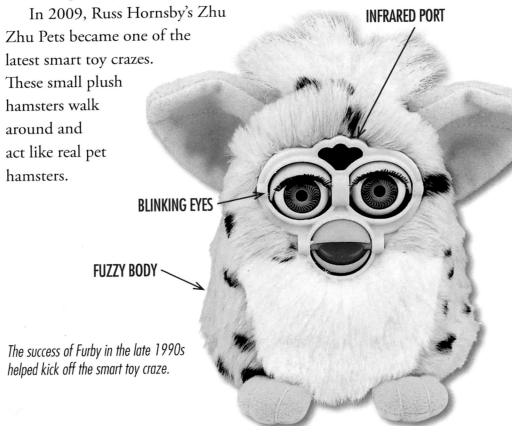

INFRARED PORT

BLINKING EYES

FUZZY BODY

The success of Furby in the late 1990s helped kick off the smart toy craze.

Mattel's Apptivity toys combine popular toys such as Hot Wheels with iPad activities and games.

iTOYS

Though it once seemed like something out of a science fiction movie, it is normal today to see someone pull a smartphone or tablet computer from his or her pocket and use it to perform some convenient function. Toys makers are taking advantage of this technology with some of their latest designs. Mattel's Apptivity toys interact with iPad apps to let kids play a variety of fun games. These toy cars and figures are equipped with special sensors that allow them to interact with the tablet's touch screen. Hot Wheels Apptivity cars are one of the most popular options. Kids can race these classic die-cast cars along a variety of virtual tracks.

Even the youngest kids are getting a chance to enjoy smartphones and tablets. Fisher-Price's Apptivity Monkey allows parents to secure an iPhone inside a soft, colorful monkey. Babies and small children can use the touch screen for fun learning activities, and the expensive electronic device is kept safe from possible damage.

FROM THIS TO THAT

Squirt gun technology has improved greatly over time.

DRIP, DRIP, DRIP

Water guns date back to the end of the 1800s. These early squirt guns consisted of a tube, a squeezable bulb, and a gun-shaped toy. When kids squeezed the bulbs, it pushed water through the tube and out of the gun. Later squirt guns were able to eliminate the bulb and tube by taking advantage of the same technology that makes spray bottles work. Kids could simply pull the squirt gun's trigger to fire it. The earliest versions of these squirt guns were made of metal, but plastic ones became more common in the mid-1900s.

THE WETTEST WEAPONS

It can be tough to cool down on a hot day. One great way to beat the heat is a water fight. For decades, kids have been tossing water balloons, spraying each other with hoses, and, best of all, blasting each other with squirt guns.

Simple plastic squirt guns do not hold a lot of water and cannot squirt very far.

Water bazookas are usually used in pools or at beaches.

BLASTING WITH BAZOOKAS

Water bazookas take a slightly different approach to summertime water combat. These plastic water guns are perfect for pools or beaches. Users stick one end of the gun underwater and then pull out the back end to suck in water. When the back is pressed in, a jet of water launches out the front of the bazooka to soak everything in its path.

ARMS RACE

Squirt gun technology underwent a huge change in 1989 when inventor Lonnie Johnson created the Super Soaker. Johnson was known for his engineering work on important space projects for NASA, but at home he tinkered with other inventions for fun. While working on one of these home projects, Johnson found that an air pump could blast water from a hose at high speed. He applied the technology to a high-powered squirt gun. Johnson sold the Super Soaker plans to Larami toys, and the squirt guns hit stores in 1990. Since then, more than 200 million Super Soakers have been sold. ✳

Air-powered squirt guns can squirt a focused jet of water.

TREMENDOUS TABLETS

Many toy companies are making tablet computers that are just for kids. They are made of durable plastic and cost far less than most other tablets. This makes them a good choice for small children who might damage a more expensive device. Just like iPads or Android tablets, LeapFrog's LeapPad and VTech's Innopad devices feature a touch screen, a microphone, and a built-in video camera. Kids can use the tablets to play games, listen to music, watch videos, and read interactive e-books.

The MEEP! tablet, by Oregon Scientific, is designed for slightly older kids. It is an actual Android tablet that can connect to the Internet and download a variety of fun and educational apps. Users can even buy accessories such as a drum pad or a keyboard to compose their own music.

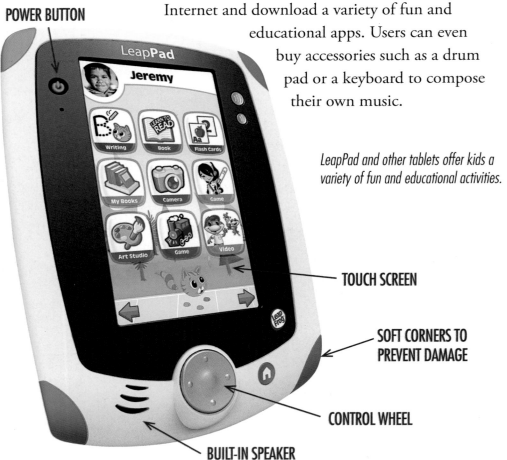

POWER BUTTON

TOUCH SCREEN

SOFT CORNERS TO PREVENT DAMAGE

CONTROL WHEEL

BUILT-IN SPEAKER

LeapPad and other tablets offer kids a variety of fun and educational activities.

CUTTING-EDGE CLASSICS

Since their debuts decades ago, Lego blocks and Barbie dolls have remained among the most successful toys in the world. But that doesn't mean that they haven't changed at all. In 1998, Lego introduced a new line of programmable robotic pieces called Mindstorms. Users can build robots using Lego pieces, then program them to perform a variety of actions. The latest version, called Lego Mindstorms NXT 2.0, was released in 2009. It contains special Lego pieces that can sense touch, motion, and color, and it also has several different motors. Users can combine these pieces with standard Lego pieces to create their own incredible robots.

One of Mattel's most recent Barbie creations is the Barbie Photo Fashion doll. This Barbie wears a special T-shirt with an LCD screen built into it. Users can plug the doll into their computers to create new graphics that display right on Barbie's T-shirt.

SENSOR EYES

PROGRAMMABLE MINDSTORMS COMPUTER AND MOTOR

GEARS FOR LEG MOVEMENT

Lego Mindstorms allow users to build their own robots and program them to perform complex actions.

MODERN MARVEL

TAKE TO THE SKIES

Action figures and video games collided like never before with the 2011 release of *Skylanders: Spyro's Adventure. Skylanders* is an action-packed video game that lets players control characters based on collectible action figures. Each action figure contains a special computer chip. When the figure is placed on a "portal" attached to the video game system, the character appears in the game for the player to control. Each character has different in-game abilities, allowing players to get a new game experience with each action figure.

BUILDING CHARACTER

As players battle enemies in the virtual *Skylanders* world, their characters earn gold and upgrades for their abilities. They also grow more powerful. All of this progress is stored on the action figure's computer chip. If the player reaches a tough part of the game with one of the characters, he or she can switch to one of the stronger action figures.

Skylanders characters appear in the video game world when they are placed on the Portal of Power.

Skylanders games have been released for several video game consoles, including the PlayStation 3, Wii, Xbox 360, and Nintendo 3DS.

ON THE GO

Because each character's progress is stored inside the action figure, players can take their favorite characters along for the ride when they go to visit friends. Two players can join forces with their own figures to battle computer-controlled enemies. They can also go head-to-head in a competition to see who has the stronger character.

CRAZY COLLECTORS

Skylanders fans go crazy for the game's collectible figures. When new characters are released, toy stores are often swarmed with fans who want to get the latest models. Some figures are more difficult to find than others, and some are only available at certain stores. This makes finding the new toys a game of its own! In 2012, a sequel called *Skylanders: Giants* was released. Of course, the new game also saw the release of new action figures, once again driving fans into a frenzy to find their favorites on toy store shelves. ✳

Fans have purchased more than 100 million Skylanders figures since the series launched in 2011.

THE NEW GIRLS IN TOWN

Barbie has long been one of the most popular dolls around, but she isn't the only girl that kids want to hang out with these days. The first three American Girl dolls were made available in 1986, and their popularity has grown incredibly ever since. The dolls were originally created to teach girls about different periods of American history. Each doll came with a life story and clothing to reflect the time period she came from. Later, dolls with modern clothing were introduced, making the line more popular than ever. Today, millions of girls flock to American Girl Place stores, where they can purchase clothing, furniture, and other accessories for their dolls. By 2008, American Girl dolls were among the most popular toys in the United States.

MATCHING OUTFITS

DOLL-SIZED TEACUP

American Girl Place stores feature restaurants where doll owners can dine with their dolls.

PLEASANT ROWLAND

American Girl dolls were created by educator Pleasant Rowland. Rowland hoped that the dolls would encourage kids to learn about history. After her huge success with American Girl, Rowland sold the company in 2000. Since then, she has devoted herself to **philanthropy**.

ROBOTS IN DISGUISE

Have you ever stood in a toy store, trying to decide between two different toys? Should you get a truck or an action figure? An airplane or a helicopter? Transformers make choices like these much easier. They are two toys in one!

Originally introduced in 1984, Transformers are some of the most famous toys ever created. Each one is a robot action figure that folds up to form a different object. Some transform into vehicles, while others take the shape of animals. Unlike other action figures, they vary widely in size. Some are only a few inches tall, while others are several times larger. Transformers became more popular than ever in 2007, with the release of a hit movie based on the characters. The toys have also inspired comic books and cartoons, and thousands of fans come together every year for conventions where they can meet the toys' creators and trade rare Transformers.

New Transformers toys based on the movie Transformers: Dark of the Moon *were released in 2011.*

Toy inventor Michael McGinnis showed off his 3D maze, Perplexus, at Toy Fair 2010. Toy inventors bring their creations to Toy Fair events in the hope that they will gain attention and become popular hits.

CHAPTER THREE

ON THE JOB

I t is not easy to succeed in the toy industry. Creating the next big thing takes a combination of creativity, hard work, and pure luck. In many other industries, consumers are always looking for the latest and greatest new things. Most people would rather play the latest video games than classics from years past. When people buy computers, they try to get the newest, fastest ones they can afford. But with toys, many of the biggest sellers are the same types of things that people have been playing with for years. Very few new toys reach the same heights of popularity. Sometimes a toy designer might have a great idea, but it might not catch on among toy buyers. To prevent this from happening, toy makers put a lot of hard work into every new creation.

DARING DOLLS

1890	1959	1986	2010
Inventor Thomas Edison begins selling the world's first talking dolls.	Barbie is released, popularizing dolls that are shaped like adults instead of babies.	The first American Girl dolls are released exclusively through the company's catalog.	Mattel introduces its Monster High dolls, which feature designs based on popular movie monsters.

Engineering classes provide students with the skills they will need to create tomorrow's most amazing innovations.

AN EDUCATION IN ENGINEERING

Very few universities have programs for designing toys. Some art schools offer classes on toy design, but students cannot pursue full degrees in the subject. Instead, virtually all future toy makers enroll in engineering programs when they go to college. Engineering is the process of designing and building things. Different branches of the field specialize in different aspects of this process. However, all engineers have some background in science and math. They learn how to solve problems and use a variety of tools and materials. These skills come in handy when building the next hit toy.

FROM DREAM TO DESIGN

Before a team of engineers can build a new toy, they need an idea to work from. New ideas come from toy designers. Designers rely on creativity to be successful. They are always thinking about possibilities for new toys or ways to improve older versions of toys. Sometimes they join forces with other designers to brainstorm ideas. Once a designer has a good idea, he or she sketches out a rough illustration of what the product might look like. Sometimes the designer draws these plans by hand. Other times, he or she uses computer software to create 3D models. These early drafts are the first step on the road to creating a toy kids will love.

Toy designers often use computers to develop their ideas for new products.

AN INTERVIEW WITH TOY DESIGNER NATE LAU

Nate Lau is a toy designer at Tegu, a company that creates magnetic wooden block toys. Tegu uses tropical hardwood from the nation of Honduras and plants trees to replace the ones that are cut down for use in its toys. Its blocks are designed to have shapes that encourage creativity in kids.

When did you realize you wanted to design toys? For as long as I can remember, I have enjoyed drawing and could often be found with a pencil in hand. Little sketches of planes or cars and sometimes just completely random doodles would find their way onto the margins of my homework, my tests, and even my desks at school. Who would have thought those doodles would end up becoming a real thing?

What kinds of things did you study or work on to prepare for your career? At first I pursued a career in architecture but soon realized that the gigantic scale of the projects was a little overwhelming. I preferred to work on things that I could hold in my hands, and product design allows you to do that. Although I'm in toy design right now, a toy is just a specialized type of product. I never thought I'd be working for a toy company when I was growing up, but it all started with my love for drawing!

Are you ever surprised by how children apply their own ideas to your toys? We love seeing kids play with our blocks. I'm never surprised by what they come up with, because I expect kids to be wild and creative! That's what kids do best!

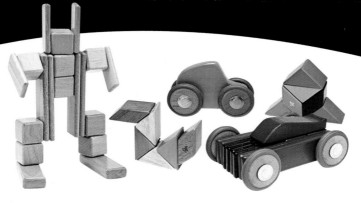

Once you have an idea for a new toy, what factors must you consider before you move forward? Tegu's purpose is to be known for excellent products that make sense while being beautifully designed. We have also made a commitment to supporting the country of Honduras and its environment by locating our factory there, creating jobs, and **repopulating** the forest. And, of course, there's our goal of utilizing new and old materials to be as environmentally **sustainable** as possible.

It takes an entire team to bring a toy from idea to completion. Does working as part of a team come naturally to you, or was it something you had to learn? When you spend your childhood hunched over a piece of paper with a pencil in hand, you don't gain many useful skills for working in a team. The good news is that design school has a way of opening your eyes and ears to other opinions and making it second nature to seek out additional views from people like you, and people who are completely different.

As an adult, how do you get yourself to think like a child while still keeping the technical side of your job in mind? I think when you become a professional designer, the difficulty comes in reminding yourself that it's OK to be a kid at times. Accessing the inner child is no problem as long as you remember that it's alright, and even encouraged.

Do you have an idea for your ultimate toy? What would you create if you had all the time and resources in the world? Now that Tegu offers magnetic wheels so kids can build their own cars to their own design with a simple pull and click, I think about how awesome it would be if there was a full-sized version to build your own pedal car or soapbox racer and customize it to your liking.

What advice would you give to a young person who wants to design toys one day? Keep drawing, anything, anywhere. Practice really does make perfect, but it won't seem like practice if it's something you enjoy. Nobody said work can't be fun. ✳

INVENTING THE INGREDIENTS

Take a look at the objects around you. Every item made by humans is made up of a variety of raw materials. Your clothes might be made of cotton or wool. This book was made using paper. More complicated items like toys might be made using a number of different materials, such as plastics, metals, or woods. Each material has its own particular strengths and weaknesses. Some plastics are more flexible than others, for instance, and some metals are easier to mold into small shapes.

Materials engineers are in charge of creating and choosing these materials. Sometimes they create brand new types of plastic for more durable toys. Other times, they might look for a metal that is just the right hardness for a certain project. They also create new methods for molding materials into different shapes, and test the materials in toys to be sure they are not poisonous or otherwise harmful. A strong background in chemistry and physics gives them the knowledge they need to excel.

A materials engineer might examine many different kinds of plastic before choosing the right one for a certain toy.

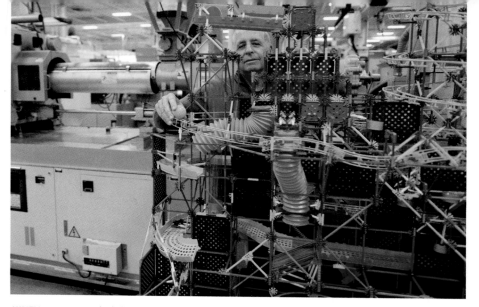

K'NEX inventor Joel Glickman relied on careful planning and engineering to create his complex building toys.

MAKING MOVEMENT WORK

Some of today's most popular toys are complex mechanical devices. They are made up of many small, moving parts, and often rely on motors or other internal mechanisms to work properly. It is up to mechanical engineers to ensure that a toy's many components all work together properly.

During the development process, mechanical engineers analyze the toy's design and decide how best to accomplish the team's goals. For example, a designer might want an action figure's arms to move in a certain way when a button on the toy's back is pressed. Mechanical engineers examine the shape of the toy and design a mechanism that will produce the arm motion the designer had in mind. If a designer wants to build a toy airplane that glides when someone throws it, mechanical engineers use their knowledge of physics to figure out how the plane should be shaped and how heavy it should be. Problem solving is the name of the game for these clever creators.

THE ARTISTIC SIDE

THE POWER OF PACKAGING

When it comes to selling big in the toy industry, a toy's packaging is almost as important as the toy itself. Artists and **marketing** experts work together to create boxes, wrappers, and other types of packaging that will capture the attention of kids and parents alike.

FINDING AN AUDIENCE

Toy packaging serves several purposes, but the most important one is drawing in customers. Artists use packaging to make a toy look as fun and exciting as possible. They include images of the toy in action, along with bright colors and exciting phrases.

Plastic toy packaging allows customers to get a look at the product while ensuring that small pieces are not lost or damaged on the way to store shelves.

They also try to make sure the packaging will appeal to the types of people they think will buy the toy. For example, the boxes that Barbie dolls come in are often bright shades of pink and purple, which are likely to draw in young girls. When packaging features photos of children using the toys, designers must make sure that the kids in the photos are around the same age as the kids who will buy the toy. Older kids won't want a toy if they think it is made for babies!

Stuffed animals are often sold in packages that allow shoppers to feel the toys before purchasing them.

HANDS ON

Many toy packages give potential customers a chance to take some of the toy's most impressive features for a test-drive. Small holes might let kids reach a finger inside to press a button and hear the toy talk. Many dolls come in packaging that leaves almost the entire toy open to touch. Getting to see and handle the toy up close can encourage people to buy it.

TO THWART A THIEF

Toy packaging is also designed to help prevent people from stealing the toys from stores. One way to avoid theft is to put small toys in large packages. For example, action figures and die-cast cars are often very small. A thief could easily put them in his or her pocket and leave the store. But most of these small toys are encased in a type of packaging known as a blister pack or clamshell packaging. This is a small bubble of plastic that is attached to a larger piece of cardboard. Because the cardboard is large, the toy is more difficult to steal. It also gives artists more room for eye-catching designs! ✳

Blister packs make small toys more difficult for thieves to place in their pockets or purses.

Many modern toys are packed with computer chips and other electronic components.

TOY TECHNOLOGY

Because so many modern toys are built using computer technology and electronic devices, computer and electrical engineers have come to play a major role at many toy companies. Computer engineers understand the ins and outs of designing and building computer systems using a variety of hardware components. If a toy has any sort of microchip or more complex computer system inside, a computer engineer likely designed it.

Electrical engineers specialize in electricity and power sources. They play a role in creating even the simplest electronic toys. For example, an electrical engineer might design the system that powers a battery-operated robot or a rechargeable tablet computer.

PROGRAMMING PLAYTHINGS

Computer hardware doesn't do much good if there is no software to control it. Software engineers and programmers work together to create the programs that tell a toy's hardware what to do. Software engineers begin by determining what kind of computer program the toy needs. They then create a plan for building that software. One way they do this is by creating flowcharts to illustrate the various functions the software will need to perform in different situations.

If the toy company has a separate team of programmers, the engineer will provide them with a plan and supervise as they write the code using a computer language. At other companies, software engineers do the programming themselves.

This shape is called a terminator. It is used to mark the first and last steps of a process.

Rectangles are used to represent steps of a process.

Diamonds are used to indicate decision points.

Yes

No

This would be the step taken if the decision was "yes."

This would be the step taken if the decision was "no."

An answer of "no" could lead to an extra step before the process is complete.

Flowcharts use a variety of shapes to outline the steps in a complex process. Here is an example of a very simple flowchart.

Another terminator shape marks the end of the chart.

BRIGHT COLORS ATTRACT SHOPPERS' ATTENTION.

SALESPEOPLE HELP ANSWER CUSTOMERS' QUESTIONS.

WIDE AISLES GIVE KIDS PLENTY OF ROOM TO MOVE AROUND AND LOOK AT THE TOYS.

ENDCAPS OFFER THE MOST VISIBILITY TO SHOPPERS.

Similar toys are grouped together at toy stores, with the latest and most popular playthings placed at the end of aisles, where they are most easily seen.

CHAPTER FOUR

A TOY'S TIMELINE

The toy industry can be extremely competitive, with companies constantly battling for toy buyers' attention and money. As soon as one toy company has a hit on its hands, others rush to catch up and release similar toys in order to take advantage of the trend. This high level of competition from rival companies pressures toy makers to get their product out on time. As one Hasbro executive put it, "In this business, if you're not there first, you're not there."

Toy creators get to see their work come together quickly. A product goes from the idea stage to store shelves in 6 to 12 months. Toy companies call this period time to market. A design that lands on an engineer's desk in July may be the hit toy of the next holiday season.

LEGENDARY TOY STORES

1760	1870	1948	1992
Hamleys toy store is founded in London, England.	Frederick August Otto Schwarz opens the shop that will eventually become the world famous FAO Schwarz toy store.	Charles P. Lazarus opens Children's Bargain Town, which is later renamed Toys"R"Us.	The first Lego retail store is opened at the Mall of America in Bloomington, Minnesota.

Toy designers might present their ideas to coworkers using drawings or charts.

GOOD IDEAS

All toys begin with an idea. Where that idea comes from, however, can be very different depending on the type of toy being created and what kinds of companies are involved. Sometimes it might be as simple as a designer having a sudden inspiration for a brand-new product. Other times, toy company executives might ask a team of designers to improve one of their old products or create new toys based on an upcoming movie.

Once designers put together rough plans for a new toy, they must seek approval before moving forward. A design team at the toy giants Mattel or Hasbro has to impress decision makers inside the company. Designers at a company that makes toys for fast-food kids' meals or cereal boxes, on the other hand, must please the clients who have hired them.

Other toy designers are independent and do not have to answer to anyone. They come up with a unique idea and then move forward with the project on their own. This is how such legendary toys as Super Soakers and Beanie Babies were created.

PLAYING WITH PROTOTYPES

Once a design is approved, toy makers must turn their rough drawings into a physical object. This first version of a toy is known as a **prototype**. A prototype is a functioning model of the toy, but it is far from a final product. It is usually built using whatever materials happen to be available. Scraps from previous toy designs, spare computer parts, and homemade pieces can all be found in early prototypes. Designers and engineers can use these early models to quickly see whether or not certain planned features will work. If there are major problems, the team might have to make some adjustments or even start over from scratch.

A prototype of an action figure might be uncolored or lack other details that the final product will have.

WHERE THE MAGIC HAPPENS

Professor David Wallace (right) is one of the instructors of the Toy Product Design class at MIT.

TOY SCHOOL

The Massachusetts Institute of Technology (MIT) in Cambridge, Massachusetts, and the University of Minnesota (UMN) in Minneapolis, Minnesota, are two of the many schools that are training tomorrow's toy makers. Students who attend these two universities are able to take a class called Toy Product Design. Students enrolled in the class break up into five- or six-person teams led by mentors and instructors. Each team's goal is to design and build a toy prototype.

THE STARTING LINE

Each team must start its project from scratch. The members begin by brainstorming ideas for their toys. They think about what kinds of toys people might actually want to buy. They also consider whether they will have the time and resources to complete the project by the end of the semester. Like professional toy designers, they sketch out rough ideas on paper and then create more detailed drawings to use as **blueprints** for the prototype.

One group of students in the 2012 UMN class created a toy called Stack Track. Wooden blocks can be stacked to create winding pathways for marbles.

PUTTING IT TOGETHER

Once the team members have settled on an idea and drawn up plans, they can begin the process of actually building their toy. Because they are all engineering students, they have the background knowledge they need in order to select materials, solve problems, take measurements, and assemble a working toy. If they run into especially difficult issues, they can consult their instructors for guidance.

THE BIG SHOW

By the end of the semester, each team must have a working prototype to present. The class then holds an event known as PLAYsensation. There, the students' creations are shown off to professors, professional toy designers, and the most important critics of all—children!

TONS OF TOYS

The toys shown off at PLAYsensation events are often very impressive. Students have built everything from a motorized skateboard to a remote control pirate boat with a built-in water cannon. Other students have designed art toys, musical instruments, and unique stuffed animals.

Students in the 2009 MIT class created a device that projects instructions for folding origami onto pieces of paper.

During play testing, toy designers watch to see how kids react to new toy designs.

TAKING TOYS FOR A TEST-DRIVE

Once the toy makers are confident that their prototype will work, the toy can move along in the production process. The company's testing department invites groups of children to try out its prototypes in a fun atmosphere. Specially trained employees observe the playgroups to keep an eye on how the children play with the toy. The company wants to see if children play with the toy in the way the designers planned and if they can figure out how to play with the toy without instructions. The toy must also fill its intended role. Educational toys must teach, while art toys should encourage children to be creative in fun ways.

DECISION TIME

Once a prototype has been play tested, the toy company's research and development (R&D) department judges whether it should be turned into a finished toy. If the playgroups did not play with the toy the right way or if they didn't have fun with it, the team might have to make some changes or even scrap the project.

The company also takes other issues into account when deciding whether or not to move forward with a project. They experiment with different ways to manufacture the toy and estimate how much it will cost to produce. They then weigh this information against an estimate of how popular they expect the toy to be. If they believe that the toy will be profitable, engineers can start on a final plan for the product.

Research and development departments examine prototypes to determine whether the company should manufacture a toy.

Engineers examine every detail of a new toy to look for possible flaws.

DOWN TO THE DETAILS

Once the toy company's engineers receive the go-ahead to work on a promising toy idea, they begin experimenting and looking for ways to make a fun and durable product while keeping manufacturing costs as low as possible. Different kinds of engineers work on different kinds of toys.

Much of the engineers' work takes place on computers. Special software allows them to experiment with different parts and materials without actually building a toy. For example, they can run simulations to see if a certain part will hold up against stress or snap in two. Each part is examined over and over again to make sure it can be manufactured easily and inexpensively. In addition, a part must hold up through years of play.

REDUCING RISKS

Safety is an important issue when designing toys. This is especially true for toys made for younger children. Engineers must take many factors into account when testing toy designs for safety. They must consider every possibility for injury. Does the toy have sharp pieces that can cut kids? Are there moving parts that could trap fingers or hair? Special software allows engineers to determine whether a toy will shatter if pounded on a table or if it could possibly suffocate a child. Every company has a program that simulates a child's throat to make sure no single part can be swallowed or cause the child to choke. For example, small holes were added to the plastic heads of Lego minifigures in recent years. These holes allow a child to continue breathing if he or she accidentally gets one of the plastic heads stuck in his or her throat. Engineers also ensure that none of the toy's materials are poisonous, in case a child puts the toy in his or her mouth.

Toys that break easily can pose a threat to young children who might injure themselves on the broken parts.

LASTING CONTRIBUTIONS

STAYING POWER

Some kinds of toys never go out of style. Kids have been playing with simple wooden toys for thousands of years. Even with the popularization of cheap, easily moldable plastics in the 20th century, wooden toys never went away completely.

KEEPING IT SIMPLE

Some parents purchase wooden toys for their children because they believe the toys encourage creative thinking. The children can use their imaginations to turn simple block shapes into cities, castles, or alien worlds. More modern toys usually have very specific shapes, which give kids fewer options when they are playing.

The simple shapes and bright colors of wooden blocks never go out of style.

ALL NATURAL

Wooden toys are also more environmentally friendly than plastic toys. Though trees must be cut down to obtain wood, trees can be regrown. Many wooden toy companies even take responsibility for replanting trees themselves. Plastic is usually made using oil, which is a limited resource found beneath the planet's surface. The world's oil supply is limited, and it cannot be regrown when it is used.

Tegu's environmentally friendly blocks use magnets to stick together.

Replanting trees can help make up for the damage caused by harvesting wood for toys and other products.

OLD TOYS, NEW MAKERS

Large toy companies such as Mattel and Hasbro do not make many wooden toys today. Instead, parents purchase these playthings from newer, smaller companies that focus exclusively on wooden toy designs. PlanToys offers a variety of wooden animals, vehicles, and games for young children. Tegu manufactures magnetic wooden blocks that can be used to build anything a child imagines. Melissa & Doug makes everything from art toys and games to pretend tools and kitchen items. ✷

```
role_id'
    'resource_id'              ➡ $role_details['id'],
    );                         ➡ $resource_details['id'],
$this->rule_exists( $resource_details['id'], $role_det
if ( $access == false ) {
    // Remove the rule as there is currently no need fo
    $details['access'] = !$access;
    $this->_sql->delete( 'acl_rules', $details );
} else {
    // Update the rule with the new access value
    $this->_sql->update( 'acl_rules', array( 'access'
}
foreach( $this->rules as $key=>$rule ) {
    if ( $details['role_id'] == $rule['role_id'] && $de
        if ( $access == false ) {
            unset( $this->rules[ $key ] );
        } else {
            $this->rules[ $key ]['access'] = $access;
        }
    }
```

During bug testing, programmers search every line of their code for errors.

THE EXTERMINATORS

Because so many toys today rely on computers, they must be carefully
tested for bugs before they can be released. Just as with any computer
software, there can sometimes be unforeseen effects once someone
actually starts using the toy. Testers play with the toy in every way they
can possibly think of, hoping to uncover any problems that software
engineers or programmers might have missed. It is very important that
any bugs are squashed before the toy is sold to the public. If the toy has a
problem that causes it to malfunction, the company might have to **recall**
it. This is an expensive and embarrassing process, and companies do
everything they can to prevent such situations from arising.

FROM FACTORY FLOOR TO STORE SHELVES

Once every aspect of the toy has been finalized, the toy company makes plans to manufacture it in large quantities. Molds and dies are created to shape the plastic and metal pieces that will be used to build the toy, and the company's factories are prepared for the manufacturing process. This can be a long, globe-spanning process. A toy company headquartered in New York City might have a plastic mold manufacturer in Osaka, Japan, and a factory in Guangzhou, China.

Once the toys have been built and are secure inside their packaging, they are shipped to toy stores. Will the new toy be the next big thing? It is up to the parents and children of the world to decide.

Toy molds are created by cutting shapes into heavy blocks of metal.

The Google Glass device places a computer screen right in front of the user's eye. Such devices could be used to create augmented reality games and toys.

WHAT'S NEXT?

When it comes to creating new concepts and building on the success of today's favorites, toy creators aren't showing any signs of slowing down. Right this minute, there is probably a designer somewhere in the world sketching out a brand-new toy, or an engineer finding a way to make an existing toy better. While we can't ever be sure what the future will hold, here are some toy trends that are likely to have a big impact in coming years.

TOYS THAT LEARN

Interactive toys are likely to become even more popular. New toys might be able to learn their owners' language, likes, dislikes, and favorite activities, and use this information to form a unique personality.

You might also start to see more interactive educational toys in classrooms. People tend to be more focused and learn better when they are doing something they enjoy. A good interactive toy could make difficult school subjects fun for children to learn.

AUGMENTED REALITY

A groundbreaking technology called **augmented** reality (AR) promises to transform the ways people play.

AR combines real-world experiences with computer-generated information. Advertisers already use AR. Today's sports fans, for example, see AR in the form of computer-generated advertisements plastered on real-life playing fields when they watch games on TV. Video game consoles and smartphones take advantage of built-in cameras to power simple AR games.

Toy creators, meanwhile, have begun combining AR with real-world toys. The tech company Qualcomm developed a storytelling prototype using Sesame Street characters. The toys in the playset feature

Tablet computers can add animated characters and backgrounds to real-world images.

The tech company Google made a splash in 2012 with an AR headset called Google Glass. Users wear the device like a pair of eyeglasses, and information is presented through a display near one eye. Such devices will be common in the near future.

GOING GREEN

As more people come to realize the importance of keeping our planet healthy and conserving natural resources, green toys are sure to grow in popularity.

Batteries are expensive to recycle. They also contain dangerous acid. The OWI toy company has created a racing car that runs on solar energy, no batteries required. Another runs on salt water. Such alternate power sources could one day become the main energy source for electronic toys.

Other toy companies have gone green by using recycled plastic and metal. Building blocks, stackable cups, and bath toys have all gotten the recycling treatment. Toysmith even sells a kit that encourages children to collect plastic grocery bags and turn the trash into a toy monster. Many companies stuff teddy bears with recycled plastic bottles. In time, many more toys might be made from recycled materials. ✳

Ernie and Bert and the furniture in their house. The same figures and furniture show up on a computer screen. Ernie and Bert speak dialogue that helps guide the child through stories and activities both on the screen and with the real-life toys.

Future AR toys will go much farther. Wearable devices will eliminate the need for smartphones or computer screens. Several companies are developing glasses that display digital information for the wearer to see.

CAREER STATS

INDUSTRIAL DESIGNERS

MEDIAN ANNUAL SALARY (2010): $58,230

NUMBER OF JOBS (2010): 40,800

PROJECTED JOB GROWTH: 10%, about average

PROJECTED INCREASE IN JOBS 2010–2020: 4,300

REQUIRED EDUCATION: Bachelor's degree in industrial design or a related field

LICENSE/CERTIFICATION: None

MATERIALS ENGINEERS

MEDIAN ANNUAL SALARY (2010): $83,120

NUMBER OF JOBS (2010): 22,300

PROJECTED JOB GROWTH: 9%, slower than average

PROJECTED INCREASE IN JOBS 2010–2020: 1,900

REQUIRED EDUCATION: Bachelor's degree in materials science or materials engineering, or a related field

LICENSE/CERTIFICATION: Most employers require a state license, available after four years of experience; test requirements vary by state

MECHANICAL ENGINEERS

MEDIAN ANNUAL SALARY (2010): $78,160

NUMBER OF JOBS (2010): 243,200

PROJECTED JOB GROWTH: 9%, slower than average

PROJECTED INCREASE IN JOBS 2010–2020: 21,300

REQUIRED EDUCATION: Bachelor's degree

LICENSE/CERTIFICATION: State license, available after four years of experience; test requirements vary by state

Figures reported by the United States Bureau of Labor Statistics

RESOURCES

BOOKS

Cunningham, Kevin. *Toys*. Ann Arbor, MI: Cherry Lake, 2009.

Hewitt, Sally. *Toys and Games*. New York: Orchard/Watts, 2004.

Kenney, Sean. *Cool Robots*. New York: Henry Holt, 2010.

Lipkowitz, Daniel. *The Lego Book*. New York: DK Children, 2012.

Ooten, Tara. *Creating the Barbie Doll: The Ruth Handler Story*. Miami: Bluewater, 2012.

Parker, Steve. *Robots for Work and Fun*. Mankato, MN: Amicus, 2011.

FACTS FOR NOW

Visit this Scholastic Web site for more information on toys:
www.factsfornow.scholastic.com
Enter the keyword **Toys**

GLOSSARY

augmented (AWG-men-tid) added to or made larger

blueprints (BLOO-prints) models or detailed plans of action

celluloid (SELL-yuh-loyd) a type of flammable plastic that was once used to manufacture toys

die-cast (DYE-kast) made using a process in which hot liquid metal is poured into a hard steel mold called a die

engineer (en-juh-NEER) someone who is specially trained to design and build machines or large structures such as bridges and roads

marketing (MAHR-kuht-ing) the practice of advertising or promoting something so people will want to buy it

micrometer (MYE-kroh-mee-tur) one one-millionth of a meter

microprocessors (MYE-kroh-prah-ses-urz) computer chips that control the functions of electronic devices

molded (MOHL-did) shaped into a particular form

philanthropy (fuh-LAN-thruh-pee) the donation of time or money to causes and charities

prototype (PROH-tuh-tipe) the first version of an invention that tests an idea to see if it will work

recall (REE-kawl) to call back a purchased product that has a defect

repopulating (ree-PAHP-yuh-lay-ting) planting new trees to replace those that have been cut down

sustainable (suh-STAY-nuh-buhl) done in a way that can be continued and that doesn't use up natural resources

vinyl (VYE-nuhl) a flexible, waterproof, shiny plastic that is used to make toys and other products

INTERVIEWING USERS
HOW TO UNCOVER COMPELLING INSIGHTS

Steve Portigal

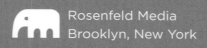

Rosenfeld Media
Brooklyn, New York

Interviewing Users: How to Uncover Compelling Insights

By Steve Portigal

Rosenfeld Media, LLC

457 Third Street, #4R

Brooklyn, New York

11215 USA

On the Web: www.rosenfeldmedia.com

Please send errata to: errata@rosenfeldmedia.com

Publisher: Louis Rosenfeld

Managing Editor: Marta Justak

Interior Layout Tech: Danielle Foster

Cover Design: The Heads of State

Copy Editor: Kezia Endsley

Indexer: Nancy Guenther

Proofreader: Dan Foster

DEDICATION

To my mom, Sharna Portigal, who taught me to ask questions.

HOW TO USE THIS BOOK

Who Should Read This Book?

This book is for everyone who talks to customers in order to do a better job of making something for them. With this book's guidance, you'll be able to gather more accurate and more finely nuanced information, whether you're a designer who brings insights into the design process, an engineer wanting to connect with how "real people" do their work, a strategist seeking a better way of identifying new opportunities, or a marketer who knows the value of data.

Even if you've never formally gone out to your users in order to inform your work, this book will guide you in the process of planning and executing a successful user research study. This book provides some very detailed best practices for studying people, and it encourages you to reflect on your own points of view.

And if you just like to ask questions, there's plenty of information here for you, too!

What's in This Book?

Chapter 1, "The Importance of Interviewing in Design," sets the stage, looking at why you learn about users and how interviewing compares with other methods.

Chapter 2, "A Framework for Interviewing," defines an approach—a way of being—for interviewing. All the tactical best practices emerge from this framework.

Chapter 3, "Getting Ready to Conduct Your Interviews," describes the steps to prepare for a user research study, from identifying the problem to finding participants and preparing your questions.

Chapter 4, "More Than Just Asking Questions," introduces a range of methods that can enhance your interviews, including artifacts you prepare and take with you, activities you ask participants to engage in, or materials you develop together with them.

Chapter 5, "Key Stages of the Interview," describes how to manage the roles of the team in the field, as well as the different stages that most interviews go through and how to prepare for and respond to those stages.

Chapter 6, "How to Ask Questions," gets into the details of asking questions, with positive and negative examples that illustrate how simple word choices can make a big difference.

Chapter 7, "Documenting the Interview," reviews how to capture all the data from interviews, the limitations (and unique strengths) of taking notes, and the necessity of a proper recording.

Chapter 8, "Optimizing the Interview," looks at common variations, typical breakdowns, and how to improve as an interviewer.

Finally, **Chapter 9**, "Making an Impact with Your Research," addresses what happens next: what you do with all that data and how to take the results back to the rest of the organization.

What Comes with This Book?

This book's companion website (rosenfeldmedia.com/books/ user-interviews/) contains a blog, sample documents, related articles, interviews, and presentations. The book's diagrams and other illustrations are available under a Creative Commons license (when possible) for you to download and include in your own presentations. You can find these on Flickr at www.flickr.com/photos/rosenfeldmedia/sets/.

FREQUENTLY
ASKED QUESTIONS

Why is this even a book? Isn't this really just talking to people? I already know how to do that!

To learn something new requires interviewing, not just chatting. Poor interviews produce inaccurate information that can take your business in the wrong direction. Interviewing is a skill that at times can be fundamentally different than what you do normally in conversation. Great interviewers leverage their natural style of interacting with people but make deliberate, specific choices about what to say, when to say it, how to say it, and when to say nothing. Doing this well is hard and takes years of practice. Chapter 6 is devoted entirely to techniques for asking questions.

Why would we bother to talk to our users? We use our products every single day and know exactly what we need to build.

People who make a product think and talk about it fundamentally differently than people who don't. While both groups may use the same product, their context—understanding, language, expectations, and so on—is completely different. From a user's point of view, a Big Mac eaten in Moscow is hardly the same product as a Big Mac eaten in San Jose, CA. And neither one is very much like a Big Mac eaten at McDonald's Hamburger University in Oak Grove, IL. A strong product vision is important, but understanding what that vision means when it leaves your bubble is make-or-break stuff. In Chapter 1, I examine the impact that interviewing has on project teams.

We don't have time in our development process to interview our users, so what should we do?

Developing insights about users doesn't always have to be a milestone in a product development process. Insights can be an organizational asset that is assembled quarterly (or whenever) to feed into all aspects of product development, marketing, and so on. Once a baseline is established, subsequent research can enhance and expand that body of knowledge. Within time constraints, I'm constantly impressed by people I meet who are so hungry to bring user information into their work that they find ways to do whatever they can. In Chapter 9, I discuss the trade-offs when time is the constraining resource.

Which team members should interview users?

While more design organizations are staffing a research role, the designated researchers aren't the only ones who go out and meet customers. I've seen many times that as companies buy in to the value of research insights, the researchers shift from struggling for acceptance to being overwhelmed by demand. It's not unusual to see them scaling up their own teams, working with outside partners, and training their colleagues to be better researchers themselves. Ultimately, who shouldn't be interviewing users? There will always be a range of strengths in interviewing skills; leading research is a specialized function, but user research is something that everyone can and should participate in. In most cases, this will exclude functions unrelated to key aspects of the business, but given the cultural value of understanding the customer, everyone could be involved in consuming the results of interviewing users, even if they aren't directly speaking to those users themselves. In Chapter 5, I look at how to manage a team composed of seasoned interviewers and less-savvy colleagues.

We interviewed users and didn't learn anything new. How does that happen?

Sometimes it's perfectly appropriate to validate hypotheses or to confirm the findings from previous research. But often when stakeholders report they didn't hear anything new, that's a symptom of something else. Were stakeholders fully involved in planning the research? Did the researchers develop a rich understanding of what these stakeholders already believed and what burning questions they had? Not hearing anything new may be a result of not digging into the research data enough to pull out more nuanced insights. Finally, if customers are still expressing the same needs they've expressed before, it begs the question, "Why haven't you done something about that?" In Chapter 3, I discuss working with stakeholders to establish project objectives.

CONTENTS

FOREWORD

I was just looking at YouTube in a brave attempt to keep in touch with popular music, and I found the musician Macklemore doing a hip-hop celebration of the thrift store. ("Passing up on those moccasins someone else been walking in.") Google results indicate that Macklemore is a product of Evergreen State University in Olympia, Washington. And this is interesting because Evergreen produces a lot of ferociously creative kids—wild things who care nothing for our orthodoxy, and still less for our sanctimony.

Now, our curiosity roused, we might well decide to go visit Evergreen College, because as William Gibson put it, "The future is already here; it's just not very evenly distributed." Evergreen would be an excellent place to look for our futures. But it wouldn't be easy or pleasant. We would struggle to get a fix on the sheer volcanic invention taking place here. Our sensibilities would be scandalized. We would feel ourselves at sea.

And that's where ethnography comes in. It is, hands down, the best method for making our way through data that is multiple, shifting, and mysterious. It works brilliantly to help us see how other people see themselves and the world. Before ethnography, Evergreen is a bewildering place. After ethnography, it's a place we "get." (Not perfectly. Not comprehensively. But the basics are there, and the bridge is built.)

And that's where Steve Portigal comes in. Armed with his method of interviewing, years of experience, a sustained devotion to the hard problems that our culture throws off (not just at Evergreen State College), and a penetrating intelligence, Steve could capture much of what we need to know about Evergreen, and he could do it in a week. And that's saying something. Steve is like a Mars Rover. You can fire him into just about any environment, and he will come back with the fundamentals anatomized and insights that illuminate the terrain like flares in a night sky. Using his gift and ethnography, Steve Portigal can capture virtually any world from the inside out. Now we can recognize, enter, and participate in it. Now we can innovate for it, speak to it, serve it.

And if this is all Steve and ethnography can do, well, that would be enough. But Steve and the method can do something still more miraculous. He can report not just on exotic worlds like Evergreen, but the worlds we know—the living room, the boardroom, the not-for-profit, and the design firm. This is noble work because we think we grasp the world we occupy. How would we manage otherwise? But, in fact, we negotiate these worlds thanks to a series of powerful, intricate assumptions. The thing about these assumptions is that, well, we assume them. This means they are concealed from view.

We can't see them. We don't know they are active. We don't know they're there. Ethnography and Steve come in here, too. They are uniquely qualified to unearth these assumptions, to discover, in the immortal words of Macklemore, *those moccasins we all go walking in.*

This is a wonderful book. Steve can teach us how to improve our ability to penetrate other worlds and examine our assumptions. Ethnography has suffered terribly in the last few years. Lots of people claim to know it, but in fact the art and science of the method have been badly damaged by charlatans and snake oil salesmen.

Let's seize this book as an opportunity to start again. Let Steve Portigal be our inspired guide.

—Grant McCracken
Chief Culture Officer, Basic Books
Culturematic, Harvard Business Review Press

INTRODUCTION

I had my first experience in user research more than 30 years ago, going on-site to classrooms and homes to see if people of various ages could tell the difference— blindfolded—between different colors of Smarties candy (a candy from Canada, where I grew up, that is similar to M&M's but with a broader color palette). It turned out that the youngest people, with their taste buds least affected by age, could tell instantly.[1]

As a tween, the initial impact of this science fair project was only on my snacking behavior. Implications for my career arc did not surface until many years later when I found myself in Silicon Valley with a fresh master's degree in HCI. This was an awkward point for me: I had no design portfolio. I hadn't conducted any usability tests. I hadn't created any interfaces. I had no design process. I had no awareness of how software (or any other product or service) was produced. All I had was a nascent point-of-view about people and technology. I was very lucky to end up working in an industrial design firm that was experimenting with actually talking to users, whether to validate design ideas or to work at the "fuzzy front-end" where innovation could take place, "left of the idea."

Even as the company was exploring how to do this sort of work, I was invited to apprentice in the emergent practice. At first, I was allowed to review videos but wasn't sent out on interviews. Then I was sent into the field but only to hold the camera and observe. Then I was allowed to ask just one or two questions at the end. And so it went. After a while, I was leading interviews myself, training other staff, and even lecturing to students and clients.

While it's tempting for me to be nostalgic about that time period as one that had a special focus on learning, I don't think anything has changed for me. Nowadays, I travel widely to interview users and to teach others how to interview users. In the past few weeks, I've led a number of training workshops and interviewed a bunch of fascinating people. (I called home from the field to report that, once again, "This is the most interesting project I've ever worked on!") Maybe it's my researcher nature, but having fresh stories from the field to share in the workshops and having refined thoughts about how to interview to take with me into the field is pretty damn wonderful.

My best wish for you is that learning about how you learn about users will fuel your own passions in some similar measure.

—Steve Portigal, March 6, 2013, Montara, California

---

1   You can read the entire research report at
     www.portigal.com/Reports/AreYouASmartie_Portigal.pdf.

The Importance of Interviewing in Design

This is a great time for the design researcher. Within user-experience design, service design, and to a lesser extent, industrial design, user research has gone from being an outsider activity, to being tolerated, to being the norm. Across industry events, conferences, online forums, school curricula, and professional practice, there's a tacit agreement that designing for the user is the preferred way to think about design. As with any generalization, there are exceptions. Maybe you aren't feeling the love right now, but you probably can agree that things are much better than they were in the past. To design for users, you must begin with a deep understanding of users. If you don't already have that understanding, you need to do some form of user research.

TIP YOU ARE NOT YOUR USER

You may be a user, but be careful of being seduced into designing for yourself. Jared Spool calls that "self design" and identifies the benefits and risks at **www.uie.com/brainsparks/2010/07/22/ uietips-self-design/**. I think he's too easy on self design. Lots of niche companies make the snowboards, outdoor equipment, and mixing gear that they, as enthusiasts, would want. But some have trouble expanding their offering in an innovative way, because they are so caught up in being the user.

NOTE GAINING INSIGHT VS. PERSUADING THE ORGANIZATION

While doing ethnographic research in Japan, I sat with my clients while they conducted another study. They brought users into a facility and showed them the most elegantly designed forms for printer ink cartridges. They were smooth, teardrop shapes that were shiny and coated with the color of the ink. They also showed users the existing ink cartridges: black rectangles with text-heavy stickers.

Can you guess what the research revealed? Of course. People loved the new designs, exclaiming enthusiastically and caressing them. Regardless of methodology, there was no insight to be gained here. I've gone back and forth about whether this was *good research* or *bad research*. It didn't reveal new information, but it provided tangible evidence to persuade someone else in the organization. This team's approach suggests that there are other issues with their design process, and while their research might have been the best solution in that situation, ideally this isn't the best use of a research study.

User Insight in the Design Process

Although there isn't a clear alignment about how much time and effort to invest and what approach to use, at least we, as user researchers, share a common goal: to gather information about users in order to support the organization when creating products, services, and more.

What I'm calling *interviewing* is also referred to by other names: user research, site visits, contextual research, design research, and ethnography, to name a few. Regardless of nomenclature, these are the key steps in the process:

- Deeply studying people, ideally in their context

- Exploring not only their behaviors but also the meaning behind those behaviors

- Making sense of the data using inference, interpretation, analysis, and synthesis

- Using those insights to point toward a design, service, product, or other solution

We go to visit our users (in their homes, their offices, their cars, their parks, and so on) most of the time, but not always. When planning a project, we ask ourselves if it's more insightful to bring participants in to see our stuff (say, prototypes we've set up in a facility meeting room) than it is for us to go out and see their stuff. Overall, our objective is to learn something profoundly new. There are points in the design process where quickly obtained, if shallow, information is beneficial, but that's not what we're focusing on here.

> **NOTE** IS THIS ETHNOGRAPHY?
>
> If you are interviewing users, are you doing *ethnography*? I don't know. What I do know is that if you refer to your use of interviewing of people as ethnography, someone will inevitably tell you that no, you aren't doing ethnography (you are doing contextual inquiry, or site visits, or in-depth interviews, and so on). The term *ethnography* seems to be particularly contentious for some folks, but...whatever! That's really their problem, isn't it? I'd rather we move on from definition wars and focus on what it is I'm getting at when I say *interviewing*—which means conducting contextual research and analyzing it to reveal a deep understanding of people that informs design and business problems.

Of course, there are varying perspectives on any "best practice." Everyone from Henry Ford to Sony to 37 Signals has offered up their reasons *not* to incorporate direct customer input into the development process. The sub-text of those claims is that people in those organizations possess an innate talent for building stuff that people love. Yet some companies that publicly make those claims have hired me to interview their users. The insights that come from studying users not only inform design but also inspire it. Across organizations, different design cultures have more or less of an appetite for inspiration or information, although in my experience it's hard to interview users without taking away a hearty dose of both.

Sometimes, the stated goal of interviewing users is to uncover their *pain points* (often known as *needs*). Embedded in this mindset is the mistaken notion that research with users is a sort of scooping activity, where if you take the effort to leave your office and enter some environment where users congregate, you'll be headed home with a heap of fresh needs. People need an X and Y, so all the designer has to do is include X and Y in their product and all will be good. What? No one really thinks that, do they? Well, take a look at Figure 1.1

Microsoft's ad campaign for Windows 7 implies an unlikely approach to research, design, and product development. The customer asks for some feature—in this case, for the OS to use less memory. Microsoft, seemingly unaware of the need—or opportunity—to optimize the memory footprint, smacks their corporate forehead as they see the light, sending their engineers scurrying to fulfill this surprising new need.

Without endlessly debating what Microsoft and their ad agency knew and when they knew it, suffice it to say that this advertisement reinforces this semi-mythical scooping model of user research.

FIGURE 1.1
Microsoft's ad for Windows 7 suggests that their approach to innovation comes from fulfilling user requests.

I'm calling it a *semi-mythical* model because this is exactly what some teams do. Although it may be better than nothing, the fact is that a lot of important information gets left behind. Insights don't simply leap out at you. You need to work hard and dig for them, which takes planning and deliberation. Further complicating the scooping model is the fact that what the designers and engineers see as "pain points" aren't necessarily that painful for people. The term *satisficing*, coined by Herbert Simon in 1956 (combining *satisfy* and *suffice*), refers to people's tolerance—if not overall embracing—of "good enough" solutions (see Figure 1.2).

Frankly, I discover satisficing in every research project: the unfiled MP3s sitting on the desktop, ill-fitting food container lids, and tangled, too-short cables connecting products are all "good enough" examples of satisficing. In other words, people find the pain of the problem to be less annoying than the effort to solve it. What you observe as a *need* may actually be something that your customer is perfectly tolerant of. Would they like all their food in tightly sealed containers? Of course. But are they going to make much effort to accomplish that? Probably not.

Beyond simply gathering data, I believe that interviewing customers is tremendous for driving *reframes*, which are crucial shifts in perspective that flip an initial problem on its head. These new frameworks (which come from rigorous analysis and synthesis of your data) are critical. They can point the way to significant, previously unrealized possibilities for design and

FIGURE 1.2
In my family room, you can see a telephone (with cord askew) stored near the floor on a VHS rack that I also use to store CDs (which don't fit) and empty CD cases. (Why am I keeping them?) Incidentally, the orange cord goes through the floor to an outdoor sump pump. And why do I even have these nearly-obsolete VHS tapes and CDs?

innovation. Even if innovation (whatever you consider that to be) isn't your goal, these frames also help you understand where (and why) your solutions will likely fail and where they will hopefully succeed. To that end, you can (and should!) interview users at different points in the development process. Here are some situations where interviewing can be valuable:

- As a way to identify new opportunities, before you know what could be designed

- To refine design hypotheses, when you have some ideas about what will be designed

- To redesign and relaunch existing products and services, when you have history in the marketplace

NOTE   THE CASE OF THE iPOD PEOPLE

Our company began working with a client after they had completed a quantitative study about where people used iPods. They had a list of top environments (such as Home, Work, In the Car, and so on), and they asked us to uncover the unmet needs that people had in those particular environments. It turned out that the specific within-environment needs people had were just not that big a deal, but what people really struggled with was moving between environments, or moving between contexts: from being alone to being in a social situation, from being stationary to being mobile, and so on. These were the real challenges for people. For example, if you've worn one earbud and let the other dangle so you could stay somewhat engaged, you've dealt with this particular issue.

So, we excitedly reported to our client that we had found the "real" problem for them to solve. We were met with uncomfortable silence before they told us that they had committed organizational resources to addressing the problem as it currently stood. In our enthusiasm, we had trouble hearing them, and for a few minutes, the conversation was tense.

Finally, we stated definitively that we *had* learned some specific things about the environments, *and* we saw a rich and complex opportunity in this new problem. And that was all it took. We delivered findings about each environment, and then we delved into the harder problem. It turns out that our client was eager to innovate, but they just needed to have their initial brief addressed. It became an important lesson for me: Reframing the problem extends it; it doesn't replace the original question.

When to Use Interviewing

There are numerous ways to gather data about users: usability testing, A/B testing, quantitative surveys, Web analytics, interviewing, focus groups, and so on. For the closest thing to a "Grand Unified Field Theory of User Research," see these examples by Elizabeth B. N. Sanders (see Figure 1.3) and Steve Mulder (see Figure 1.4). Both do a nice job of creating an organizing structure around the surfeit of research techniques we are blessed with.

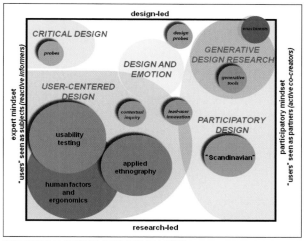

ELIZABETH B. N. SANDERS, MAKE TOOLS, LLC 2012

FIGURE 1.3
A framework for different research techniques, factoring in different philosophical approaches toward the design process and the user's role in that process.

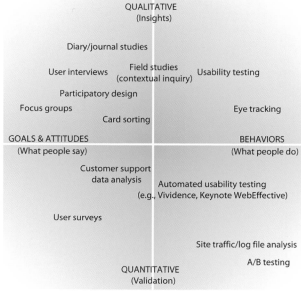

STEVE MULDER

FIGURE 1.4
Different research techniques, organized by what is being examined and which style of research objective we're addressing.

NOTE EXAMPLES OF USER RESEARCH APPROACHES

- **Usability testing:** Typically done in a controlled environment such as a lab, users interact with a product (or a simulation of a product) and various factors (time to complete a task, error rate, preference for alternate solutions) are measured.

- **A/B testing:** Comparing the effectiveness of two different versions of the same design (e.g., advertisement, website landing page) by launching them both under similar circumstances.

- **Quantitative survey:** A questionnaire, primarily using closed-ended questions, distributed to a larger sample in order to obtain statistically significant results.

- **Web analytics:** Measurement and analysis of various data points obtained from Web servers, tracking cookies, and so on. Aggregated over a large number of users, Web analytics can highlight patterns in navigation, user types, the impact of day and time on usage, and so on.

- **Focus group:** A moderated discussion with 4 to 12 participants in a research facility, often used to explore preferences (and the reasons for those preferences) among different solutions.

- **Central location test:** In a market research facility, groups of 15 to 50 people watch a demo and complete a survey to measure their grasp of the concept, the appeal of various features, the desirability of the product, and so on.

Interviewing isn't the right approach for every problem. Because it favors depth over sample size, it's not a source for statistically significant data. Being semi-structured, each interview will be unique, making it hard to objectively tally data points across the sample. Although we are typically interviewing in context, it's not fully naturalistic. A tool that intercepts and observes users who visit a website is capturing their actual behavior, but sitting with users and having them show you how they use a website is an artifice.

Interviews are not good at predicting future behavior, especially future purchase intent or uncovering price expectations. Asking those questions in an interview will reveal mental models that exist today, which can be insightful, but won't necessarily be accurate.

But interviewing can be used in combination with other techniques. In a note earlier in this chapter, I described how a quantitative study helped focus our contextual interviewing and observations. In other situations, we've used an exploratory interviewing study to identify topics for a global quantitative segmentation study. We've combined a Central Location Test (where larger groups watched a demo in a single location such as a research facility and filled out a survey) with in-home interviews simultaneously and used the results of both studies to get a deeper understanding of the potential for the product. It can be valuable to combine a set of approaches and get the advantages of each.

Is interviewing considered to be user research? Is it market research? Is it design research? I can't answer those questions any better than you can! The answer is: it depends. Whether or not you ally yourself or your methods with any one of those areas, you can still do great work uncovering new meaning and bringing it into the organization to drive improvement and growth. At the end of the day, isn't that what we care about? I'll let someone else argue about the overarching definition matrix.

To Interview Well, One Must Study

Much of the technique of interviewing is based on one of our earliest developmental skills: asking questions (see Figure 1.5). We all know how to ask questions, but if we asked questions in interviews the way we ask questions in typical interactions, we would fall short. In a conversational setting, we are perhaps striving to talk at least 50 percent of the time, and mostly to talk about ourselves. But interviewing is not a social conversation. Falling back on your social defaults is going to get you into trouble!

CHERYL PORTIGAL-TODD, 2008

FIGURE 1.5
Childhood is marked by frequent, inevitable question-asking.

Interviewing users involves a special set of skills. It takes work to develop these skills. The fact that it looks like an everyday act can actually make it harder to learn how to conduct a good interview because it's easy to take false refuge in existing conversational approaches. Developing your interviewing skills is different than developing a technical skill (say, milk-shake-machine recalibration) because you would have nothing to fall back on if learning about milkshake machines. With interviewing, you may need to learn how to override something you already know. Think of other professionals who use verbal inquiry to succeed in their work: whether it is police officers interrogating a suspect or a lawyer cross-examining an opposing witness or a reference librarian helping a patron, the verbal exchange is a deliberate, learned specialty that goes beyond what happens in everyday conversation. For you as an interviewer, it's the same thing.

The Impact of Interviewing

Interviewing creates a shared experience, often a galvanizing one, for the product development team (which can include researchers, designers, engineers, marketers, product management, and beyond). In addition to the information we learn from people and the inspiration we gain from meeting them, there's a whole other set of transformations we go through. You might call it *empathy*—say a more specific understanding of the experience and emotions of the customer—which might even be as simple as seeing "the user" or "the customer" as a real live person in all their glorious complexity. But what happens when people develop empathy for a series of individuals they might meet in interviews? They experience an increase in their overall capacity for empathy.[1]

This evolution in how individual team members view themselves, their design work, and the world around them starts to drive shifts in the organizational culture (see Figure 1.6). This capacity for empathy is not sufficient to change a culture, but it is necessary.

More tactically, these enlightened folks are better advocates for customers and better champions for the findings and implications of what has been learned in interviews.

The wonderful thing about these impacts is that they come for free (or nearly). Being deliberate in your efforts to interview users will pay tremendous dividends for your products, as well as the people who produce it.

---

1 In http://rfld.me/SzBioQ, William Hamilton Bishop describes a process for interactions between couples that sounds a lot like many of the best practices for judgment-free listening that I'll outline here. He observes that as his clients go through this process, their overall capacity for empathy increases significantly. If we substitute user interviews for the process Bishop outlines, it's good evidence that we can expect our own empathy to increase as well.

FIGURE 1.6
Team experiences that are challenging and out-of-the-ordinary create goodwill
and a common sense of purpose.

Summary

It's become increasingly common, perhaps even required, for companies
to include user research in their design and development process. Among
many different approaches to user research, interviewing (by whatever
name you want to call it) is a *deep dive* into the lives of customers.

- Interviewing can be used in combination with other techniques,
  such as identifying key themes through interviews and then vali-
  dating them quantitatively in a subsequent study.

- At a distance, interviewing looks just like the everyday act of talking to people, but interviewing well is a real skill that takes work
  to develop.

- Interviewing can reveal new "frames" or models that flip the problem on its head. These new ways of looking at the problem are
  crucial to identifying new, innovative opportunities.

- Interviewing can be used to help identify what could be designed,
  to help refine hypotheses about a possible solution that is being
  considered, or to guide the redesign of an existing product that is
  already in the marketplace

- Teams who share the experience of meeting their users are enlightened, aligned, and more empathetic.

CHAPTER 2

A Framework for Interviewing

When Wayne Gretzky apocryphally[1] explained his hockey success as "I don't skate to where the puck is, I skate to where the puck is going to be," he identified a key characteristic of many experts: the underlying *framework* that drives everything. This platonically idealized Gretzky could have revealed any number of tactics such as his grip, or the way he shifts his weight when he skates. Keith Richards explains his guitar sound, which involves removing the 6th string, tuning to open G, and using a particular fretting pattern, as "five strings, three notes, two fingers, and one asshole." Even though Keith is explaining the tactics, he's also revealing something ineffable about where he's coming from. The higher-level operating principles that drive these experts are compelling and illustrative.

Expert researchers also have their own operating principles. In this chapter, I'll outline mine, and I hope to inspire you to develop your own interviewing framework. As you develop, the process evolves from *a toolkit for asking questions* into *a way of being*, and you'll find that many of the tactical problems to solve in interviewing are simply no-brainers. As George Clinton sang, "Free your mind...and your ass will follow."

Check Your Worldview at the Door

I've been asked, "What was the most surprising thing you ever learned while doing fieldwork?" I scratch my head over that one because I don't go out into the field with a very strong point of view. Of course, I'm informed by my own experiences, my suspicions, and what my clients have told me, but I approach the interviews with a sense of what I can only call a bland curiosity.

As the researcher, it's my responsibility to find out what's going on; I'm not invested in a particular outcome. Even more (and this is where the blandness comes from), I'm not fully invested in a specific set of answers. Sure, we've got specific things we want to learn—questions we *have* to answer in order to fulfill our brief. But my hunger to learn from my participant is broad, not specific. I'm curious, but I don't know yet what I'm curious about. My own expectations are muted, blunted, and distributed. Although I will absolutely find the information I'm tasked with uncovering, I also bring a general curiosity. Now, the people I work with don't have the luxury of bland curiosity. Whether they are marketers, product managers, engineers, or designers (or even other researchers), they often have their own beliefs about what is going on with people. This makes sense: if there's enough organizational momentum to convene a research project, someone has been thinking hard about the issues and the opportunities, and has come to a point of view.

---

1 In fact, it was Walter Gretzky, Wayne's dad, who said it, as "Go to where the puck is going, not where it has been," according to Fast Company's Consultant Debunking Unit. http://rfld.me/Rj6XpR

The Brain Dump

At the beginning of the project, convene a brain dump (see Figure 2.1). Get what's in everyone's heads out on the table. Whether it's real-time, face-to-face, in front of a whiteboard, or asynchronously across offices on a wiki, talk through assumptions, expectations, closely-held beliefs, perspectives, and hypotheses. Contradictions are inevitable and should even be encouraged. The point is not establishing consensus; it's to surface what's implicit. By saying it aloud and writing it down, the issues leave the group specifically and enter an external, neutral space.

FIGURE 2.1
Capture everything that everyone thinks they know so that it's not stuck in their heads.

It's also not about being right or wrong; I encourage you to anonymize all the input so that people don't feel sheepish about expressing themselves. I wouldn't even go back and validate the brain dump against the resulting data. The objective is to shake up what is in your mind and free you to see new things. Think about it as a transitional ritual of unburdening, like men emptying their pockets of keys, change, and wallet as soon as they return home (Figure 2.2).

FIGURE 2.2
Transitional rituals
are actions we take to
remind ourselves that
we are shifting from
one mode of being to
another.

WORK IT OUT

Chicago's DD+D (who bill themselves as "a theater-based design team") offers a Design Empathy workshop. Using improv
and other theater techniques, this workshop "helps designers
to check in and acknowledge their own biases and to explore
assumptions before going out and doing research."[2]

---

2   Touchpoint, the Service Design Network publication, Volume 4, Issue 2.

Make the Interview About the Interview

Another transitional ritual is to make a small declaration to yourself and your fellow fieldworkers in the moments before you begin an interview. If you are outside someone's apartment or entering their workspace, turn to each other and state what you are there to accomplish. If you were in a movie, you'd probably growl purposefully "Let's do this thing." Sadly, fieldwork is not quite that glamorous, so you might want to clarify what you mean by "this thing." Remember, even if you consider the fieldwork part of a larger corporate initiative to "identify next-gen opportunities for Q3 roadmap," that's not where you should be focusing as you start your interview. Set aside the underlying goals for the duration of the session. "This thing" might instead be learning about Paul and how he uses his smartphone or GlobeCorp's IT department and how they deploy new routers. It's important to take that moment to tangibly confirm—and affirm—your immediate objective.

Embrace How Other People See the World

If you've effectively purged yourself of your own worldview, you are now a hollow vessel waiting to be filled with insights. Lovely image, isn't it? It's not quite accurate. You need to not only be ready to hear your participant's take on things, but you should also be *hungry* for it. This willingness to embrace is an active, deliberate state.

Go Where the People Are

Rather than asking people to come to you to be interviewed, go where they are. In order to embrace their world, you have to be in their world. Inviting them into your realm (and let's face it, even if a neutral market research facility isn't technically *your* realm, that's how your participants will perceive it) won't cut it. You'll benefit by interviewing them in their own environment—this is the environment you are interested in, where the artifacts and behaviors you want to learn about are rooted. By the same token, you'll also benefit from your own first-hand experience in that environment. The information you learn when going into other people's worlds is different from what you learn when bringing them into yours.

To that end, try not to bring your world into theirs. Leave the company-logo clothing (and accessories) at home. Wearing your colors is fine when you're rooting for the home team or taking your hog to Sturgis, but it has no place in the interviewing room (see Figure 2.3).

FIGURE 2.3
Displaying your affiliation may be appropriate in some settings, but not typically during fieldwork.

Be Ready to Ask Questions for Which You Think You Know the Answer

You already know how *you* plan a balanced meal, prepare your taxes, or select an aspect ratio on your HDTV. You may already have an idea about how your participant does those things (because of what you've learned about them during the screening process, or implied by something they said earlier in the interview, or assumed by what you've seen other people do in the past). However, you need to be open to asking for details anyway. I'll have more to say in subsequent chapters about asking questions, but for now keep in mind that to embrace their world you need to explore the details of their world. Some people fear that they are being false by asking a question if they think they know the answer. But don't be so confident with your own presumptions. Interesting tidbits can emerge when you ask these questions, as this hypothetical example suggests:

Question: When are your taxes due?

The answer (which you already know): April 15

The response you fear: Why are you asking me this stuff? Everyone knows that it's April 15. Get out of my house, jerk face!

The type of answer you are just as likely to get if you swallow your discomfort and ask the question anyway: I always complete everything by March 1. I *think* it's April 15 this year, but I never really pay attention to that.

The goal here is to make it clear to the participant (and to yourself) that they are the expert and you are the novice. This definitely pays off. When I conduct research overseas, people tangibly extend themselves to answer my necessarily naïve questions. Although it's most apparent in those extreme situations, it applies to all interviews. Respect for their expertise coupled with your own humility serves as a powerful invitation to the participant.

Nip Distractions in the Bud

Tactically, make sure that you are not distracted when you arrive. Take care of your food, drink, and restroom needs in advance. When I meet up with colleagues who are coming to the interview from a different location, we pick an easy location (such as a Starbucks) for a pre-interview briefing. It gives us time to acclimate into interview mode, review the participant's profile, catch up on what's been happening in the field to date, and address our personal needs. If your brain is chattering, "Lord, am I famished! When's lunch?" you are at a disadvantage when it comes to tuning into what's going on in the interview.

Needless to say, silence your mobile phone and don't plan on taking calls or checking texts or emails during the interview. I say "needless," but I met a team that took a different approach. Sensitive to the commitment their internal clients were making in leaving the office for fieldwork, they allowed mobile device usage during the interview, within limits. Although they were inspired by one colleague who had the stealth-check-below-the-table move down cold, most people weren't able to handle it quite so deftly. It was a good lesson to learn; they won't be allowing cell phones in the future. Mind you, even if one were successfully stealthy, that's beside the point. Figure 2.4 is an evocative depiction of the multitasking potential of technology, but during an interview (and probably during a date), you should be fully engaged with the other person.

A connection can happen anywhere

The Nokia N800 Internet Tablet delivers the web content you need, in the moments you need it most. Stay ahead of the latest headlines, catch the games you can't miss, or stay in touch with internet calling, messaging and email. With instant Wi-Fi connectivity and a high-definition screen, you get the web experience you're used to, even in places you're not.

nseries.com/n800

The Nokia N800 Internet Tablet. Take the internet to new places.

NOKIA
Nseries

FIGURE 2.4
Just because you *can* multitask doesn't mean you *should*.

Building Rapport

I often leave an interview with my head slightly swimming, in a state between energized and exhausted. In addition to all the useful information that will impact the project, I've just made an intense connection with a new person. I've established a rapport with someone. That's a powerful feeling, and likely as not, my participant is feeling the same way. Our quotidian transaction to learn about breakfast making has turned into something else.

The rapport is what makes for great interviews. You won't leave every interview walking on a cloud, but getting to that state with your interviewee is something to strive for.

It's your job to develop that rapport over the course of the interview. By all means, recruit participants who are articulate, outgoing, and eager to be part of the interview, but remember that creating that connection falls to you, the interviewer. As in life, you'll meet some people who you'll connect with easily, and others who you'll have to work hard for. Some of my best interviews have been with people who are visibly uncomfortable or disinterested at the outset.

Be Selective About Social Graces

Your participants have no framework for "ethnographic interview," so they will likely be mapping this experience onto something more familiar like "having company" (when being interviewed at home) or "giving a demo" (when being interviewed about their work). Sometimes when you visit people in their homes, they will offer you a drink. For years, I resisted taking the drink, trying to minimize the inconvenience I was causing. I was well intentioned but naïve; one time I declined a proffered drink and met an ongoing undercurrent of hostility. The drink offer was made again, so I accepted, and suddenly everything thawed. The issue wasn't my pursuit or denial of refreshment, it was acknowledging my participant's social expectations—guests should act like guests. This experience took place in the U.S.; in other parts of the world (say, Japan), these rituals are even more inflexible and failure to adhere to them will likely doom the interview. Be sure that you're aware of the social expectations in the country in which you conduct your interviews.

In addition to accepting a drink, allow for some small talk as you get settled. But don't dwell on the chitchat, because your participant may find this confusing.

Be Selective When Talking About Yourself

You are bound to hear stories in the field that you strongly identify with, whether it's someone's frustration with a broken part of Windows or their passion for Pre-Code Hollywood. Although it's important to connect with your participant, it's not the best idea to get there by sharing your common interest. Remember that the interview isn't about you. If you also love Pre-Code Hollywood, you may think "OMG! Another fellow Pre-Code Hollywood enthusiast!" *But you don't have to say that!* Think about when to reveal something about yourself (and when not to). Putting a "me too!" out there changes the dynamic of the interview. It may work to develop some rapport in a difficult situation, or it may imply you are more interested in talking about yourself than listening to the other person. Although this approach might work in social settings, where "see how interesting I am!" is a way we establish our worth in new situations, it can be detrimental in an interview.

You should definitely talk about yourself if doing so gives the other person permission to share something. As an example, early on in my career I was part of an interview team where my role was to hold the video camera and ask only a few supporting questions. As our participant was telling us about her family and their history, she stopped and looked at both of us and said, "Well, you know, my family is Jewish." She was hesitant to continue. I piped up, explaining "My family is Jewish as well." She said to me, "Well, then you understand." She then turned to my colleague and proceeded to explain the specific details she wanted to convey. I don't always tell my Jewish interviewees, "Hey, I'm Jewish, too! I have a menorah, too!" but in this case a small revelation gave the interviewee permission to move forward with the interview.

As we rang the doorbell, my colleague and I unconsciously straightened, preparing ourselves for that all-important first impression, that moment when our research participant would come to the door and size us up. We waited for a moment, looking at each other as we heard footsteps, mustering a smile as the inside door opened.

"Hello," I offered, "Are you Brian?"

As I began to state the obvious, that we were here for the interview, he grunted, opened the screen door, and as we took hold, he turned around and walked back into the house. We glanced at each other and stepped into the foyer. What did we know about Brian? Our recruiting screener told us he was 22, lived with his parents and brother, and was employed part-time. The rest would be up to us to discover.

It was 7:30 in the morning, and we were taking our shoes off in a strange house. Eventually, someone beckoned from the kitchen, and we went in. But already we were out of sync. The kitchen was small, with an L-shaped counter and a small table for dining. Brian's mother was at the end of the L, working with bowls and dishes and burners on the stove. Brian's father was perched against the counter, while Brian and his younger brother sat at the table. His father was a small man, while the other three were quite large. The room wasn't big enough for the six of us, so we managed to set up for the interview in the only place we could—at the far end of the counter. We wedged ourselves (one behind the other) on small chairs, pulling our knees in, our paraphernalia of notepads, documents, video cameras, tapes, batteries, and so on clutched in close. It wasn't ideal, but we hoped we could make it work.

The real challenge quickly became clear: Although Brian had agreed to be interviewed, he was actively disinterested. We had recruited Brian specifically, but here we were with the entire family. We pressed ahead, explaining our study, and starting in with our planned questions. Since Brian was the person with whom we had the arrangement, we focused our attention on him. He responded with one-word answers (which sounded more like grunts) and the occasional glance at his brother, causing them both to giggle.

My colleague and I avoided looking at each other (it may not have been physically possible, given the tight quarters) for fear of displaying our despair. Sure, we had arranged this interview, but the cues we were receiving were making it clear the arrangement wasn't worth much. At this point, we had already awoken quite early to conduct this interview, so there was no point in giving up. If they changed their mind explicitly, they'd let us know, and we'd leave. Meanwhile, what else was there to do but press on? I asked questions with very little response. I tried the brother, at which point Brian bolted out of the room for a few minutes, without a word. The brother was only slightly more amenable than Brian, mostly interested in making critical comments about his parents (to Brian's great grunting enjoyment), rather than providing any actual information.

Indeed, it appeared that Brian had not informed his parents that we were coming. Although I directed some of the questioning toward his mom, she reacted with pretty serious hostility, informing us (in the context of an answer to a question) that they did not welcome strangers into their house, and (while she was preparing food) highlighted the intimate nature of food preparation as a symbol, which was even less open to strangers. The message was very clear.

But again, what could we do? Pressing on until we were specifically asked to leave, under the explicit agreement we had made, seemed the best approach. We asked our questions, following up on the information they had shared, listening closely, looking for clarification, offering up as much space as we could for them to talk, all in trying to build some flow and dialogue.

Even though the message was negative, at least the parents were willing to talk to us. And so the young men faded out of the conversation, and the interview eventually switched over to the parents. Two hours later, it turned out that we had completed an excellent interview with them; they each had great stories about our topic area and revealed a lot of background about their family, about growing up, about their activities, and even their perspectives on what made the United States the country it had become. By not giving up, by ignoring our own discomfort, and by being patient in building rapport, a near-failure turned into a triumph.

Indeed, before we left the house, the mother insisted on cooking up some fried bread, fresh and hot for us. She stated that "No one comes here and doesn't get food," thus reiterating the intimate nature of food she had mentioned at the beginning, but this time as a compliment rather than a warning.

As soon as we left the house, my colleague turned to me and said, "I don't know how you pulled that off; I thought we were done for and would have to leave." I was very pleased with how the interview turned out, especially because it began so poorly, but there was little magic to it. I didn't try to solve the big problem of the complex dynamic we had walked into; I just focused (especially at first) on the next problem—the immediate challenge of what to say next. I was certainly keeping the larger goals in mind of how to cover all the areas we were interested in, but I was focusing my energy as an interviewer on the next point. And by working at it in small pieces, bit by bit, the dynamic shifted. As interviewers, we had to compartmentalize the social experience of the event—the extreme discomfort and awkwardness of the early part of the interview—and stick to our jobs. We didn't handle the situation that differently than any other interview, and it served as a testament to our approach—listening, following up (and showing that we were listening by the way we followed up), building rapport and trust bit by bit, until there was a great deal of openness and great information.

Looking back on this experience years later, it's obvious that there are better ways to communicate with the participants ahead of time to screen out the unwilling. I should have spoken directly to the person we were visiting before the day of the interview, in order to get that person-to-person communication started early. But, given the diversity of people, there's still a good chance that you'll end up with someone sometime who isn't initially comfortable with the interview process, and it's your job to make them comfortable. Doing so may make you uncomfortable, but with practice, you'll learn to set aside social dynamics and focus on the question asking and listening that will make the interview a success. See Chapter 8, "Optimizing the Interview," for more on troubleshooting this type of common interview problem.

Work Toward the Tipping Point

There's often a visceral point in the interview where the exchange shifts from a back-and-forth of *question-and-answer, question-and-answer* to a *question-story* setup. It's such a tangible shift in the interview that I feel as if I can point to it when it happens. Stories are where the richest insights lie, and your objective is to get to this point in every interview.

The thing about this tipping point is that you don't know when it's coming. So you have to be patient in the question-and-answer part of the interview because you don't necessarily know that what you're doing to build rapport is getting you anywhere. You have to trust in the process, which is easier with experience.

Acknowledge That the Interview Is…Something Unusual

Although your participants are using "social call" or "vendor meeting" as their initial framework for their experience with you, it's not a perfect model. Strangers don't typically visit us and take video of us grinding coffee beans. Falling back on naturalistic observation is disingenuous; it's not easy for participants to pretend you aren't there and just go on as they would normally. If we make the generous assumption that people on reality TV shows are in fact behaving naturally, that is typically due to an extensive amount of time surrounded by cameras, where what is *natural* shifts to something different. You won't have enough time in your interview to accomplish that. Instead, leverage the constructed nature of your shared experience. You are empowered to ask silly-seeming detailed questions about the mundane because you are joined together in this uncommon interaction. Frame some of your questions with phrases such as "What I want to learn today is…" as an explicit reminder that you have different roles in this shared, unnatural experience.

Listening

When you engage in conversation, you're often thinking about what you want to say next and listening for the breathing cues that indicate it's your turn to speak. As you jockey for your 51% of the conversation space, listening becomes a limited resource. Although we all like to consider ourselves "good listeners," for interviewing you must rely on a very special form of listening that goes beyond the fundamentals, such as "don't interrupt."

Listening is the most effective way you can build rapport. It's how you demonstrate tangibly to your participants that what they have to say is important to you.

Listen by Asking Questions

In addition to demonstrating listening by what you *don't* say, you can also demonstrate that you are listening by what you *do* say. The questions you ask are signifiers that you are listening. Try to construct each question as a follow-up to a previous answer. If you are following up on something other than what the participant just said, indicate where your question comes from. For example, "Earlier, you told us that…" or "I want to go back to something else you said…." Not only does this help the person know that you're looping back, it also indicates that you are really paying attention to what they are telling you, that you remember it, and that you are interested. If you are going to change topics, just signal your transitions: "Great. Now I'd like to move on to a totally different topic."

Be Aware of Your Body Language

Make and maintain eye contact with your participant. If you find eye contact personally challenging, take breaks and aim your gaze at their face, their hands, and items they are showing you. Use your eyes to signal your commitment to the interview. Acknowledge their comments with head nods or simple "mm-hmm" sounds. Be conscious of your body position. When you are listening, you should be leaning forward and visibly engaged (see Figure 2.5). When you aren't listening, your body tells that story, too (see Figure 2.6).

FIGURE 2.5
Good listening body language.

FIGURE 2.6
Not so much.

The listening body language is important because it not only gets you in the state, or reflects the state that you're in, but it also very clearly tells the person you're talking to that you are listening.

If your brain is listening, your body will naturally follow. But it works the other way, too! Just as therapists and life coaches encourage people to "act as if," you can also put your body into a listening posture and your brain will follow. Consider the example described by Malcolm Gladwell in his article *The Naked Face*. He describes the work of psychologists who developed a coding system for facial expressions. As they identified the muscle groups and what different combinations signified, they realized that in moving those muscles, they were inducing the actual feelings. He writes:

> Emotion doesn't just go from the inside out. It goes from the outside in...In the facial-feedback system, an expression you do not even know that you have can create an emotion you did not choose to feel.

TIP **FEEDBACK IS BACK**

If you are recording your interviews on video for later editing, you may find the "mm-hmm" noises incredibly aggravating. Unless you are miking your participants, your affirmations may be much louder than their responses (see Figure 2.7). For novice interviewers in particular, it's still good to let the "mm-hmm" fly and really work on developing rapport, even if the resulting video is going to suffer a bit. It's better to have abrupt audio changes in the deliverable than fail to achieve the maximum possible rapport in the interview. As you gain experience interviewing, learn to silently affirm with facial expressions and head-nods, and throw in the vocalization only occasionally.

FIGURE 2.7
The interviewer's affirmations can be louder than the participant's comments.

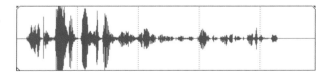

Summary

Experts have a set of best practices—tactics, really—that they follow. But what really makes them expert is that they have a set of operating principles. This looks more like a framework for how *to be,* rather than a list of what *to do.* You will have your own framework, but mine consists of the following:

- Check your worldview at the door. When you begin fieldwork, don't fixate on what you expect to learn, but rather cultivate your own general, non-specific curiosity.

- Embrace how other people see the world. Do your fieldwork in their environments—not in yours. Before you head out to the field, get the team together and do a cleansing brain dump of all the things you might possibly expect to see and hear, leaving you open to what is really waiting for you out there.

- One of the factors that makes for great interviews is the rapport that you establish between you and your participant. Don't forget that it's up to you to build that rapport. Focus on them and be very selective about talking about yourself.

- Your job is to listen beyond "Keep your mouth shut and your ears open." Your choice of questions and how you ask them demonstrate that you are listening. Pay attention to how your body language cues your participant—and you—as to how well you are paying attention.

CHAPTER 3

Getting Ready to Conduct Your Interviews

Anyone who has ever painted a room knows all too well the amount of time it takes to prepare before you ever brush a single stroke— you have to tape off windows and trim, move the furniture, spread out the drop cloths, and so on. Sometimes I find this preparation tedious and unrewarding (I wanna see paint on the wall!), but I also know from experience that all the prep work has a dramatic impact on the quality and efficiency of the painting process itself. I know you see this coming, but here it is: Interviewing users requires the same level of prep work. There's a significant amount of preparation involved before you begin asking the users anything. This may make some teams anxious if they've assumed the launch of a research project means fieldwork tomorrow. But these projects are by nature vaguely defined. You probably don't know what you don't know, which is why you are using interviews as your research method. The time spent creating alignment and developing a plan pays off tremendously.

In this chapter, I'll review the key issues to address when putting together a study, including who to interview (and where to find them), uncovering specific goals and defining the technique that will help address those goals, and refining the basic logistics that will make your time in the field go smoothly.

Establishing Your Objectives

Clarifying the objectives—what you hope to get out of the research—is an extremely challenging aspect of many engagements. Even though I begin capturing objectives in the initial conversations with the client, when it's only a potential project, the objectives are further clarified while we are planning the research, executing the study, and even up until the delivery of results. Sometimes the objectives are not a fit for the approach. Researchers are often asked to find out how much participants would pay for a product, often when that product doesn't yet exist. Reponses to that question will not be valid, and it's good to clarify for stakeholders as early as possible the limitations of contextual research (or any research method, for that matter).

At the outset of a project, make the objectives your initial priority. The first interviews you conduct should be with the stakeholders—these are often consumers of the research findings who are less likely to be involved in the day-to-day study. I typically aim for 6–8 stakeholders, although some clients ask for twice that amount. These are one-on-one conversations either on-site or on the phone. They run between 30 and 60 minutes and are used to dig deeper into objectives and establish collaboration. You should ask the stake-holders about:

- History with the organization and the research topic
- Current beliefs about the customer, the user, and the proposed solution
- Organizational or other barriers to be mindful of
- Business objectives for the project and specific questions the research should answer
- Concerns or uncertainty around the methodology

You should also review other material, such as previous research reports, existing products, and in-development prototypes.

Even though what you're learning will undoubtedly inform all of the activities throughout the project, the immediate output is the research goals—articulating what you want to learn from the interviews.

On a project that dealt with reviewing products and services online, the team arrived at five research goals. Here's one of them:

> *Structure of Social Network.* How is decision-making driven by the structure of people's social network (on and offline)?

> More specifically:

> - What do people's social networks look like? What tools do they use and how are their networks structured?
> - How do people leverage social networks for shopping and other kinds of decision-making? Who has influence with them currently?
> - Who among their social network (and beyond) are trusted sources of information for various decisions and purchases (particularly within the client's area of business)?

My team created a document that summarized the project as we understood it at the time, including the agreed-upon methodology and the complete set of five research goals. I shared this document with our client to ensure that we were aligned. In most cases, the goals come easily and are not controversial. In rare cases, the goals may be wide-ranging and exceed the planned scope of investigation. In some cases, the goals are not a good fit for the approach you are planning. Use this checkpoint to realign, reprioritize, or expand the work.

by Nate Bolt and Cyd Harrel

Nate Bolt is a design research manager at Facebook. Previously, he was CEO of Bolt | Peters and an adjunct professor at SVA iXD.

Cyd Harrell is an advisor to Code for America and other civic projects. She was previously VP of UX Research at Bolt | Peters.

There are two ways to approach a road trip. At one extreme, you can just go. At another, you can spend months planning the whole thing. Which approach will lead to a deeper exposure to the region you're traveling in? It's certainly open to debate, and the same can be true of planning user research.

FIGURE 3.1
Nate Bolt, UX Research Manager, Facebook

From our time at Bolt | Peters, we're fans of minimal preparation for research because it allows for maximum serendipitous revelations and maximum speed. We frequently do successful interview studies with a single day of preparation, and that includes plenty of time for lunch. For start-up clients, we can then complete the research and generate useful recommendations in one more day. Some researchers would call this reckless and irresponsible, but we don't think so. For us, it's efficient, realistic, and fun.

FIGURE 3.2
Cyd Harrell, Citizen Experience Advocate

An Example: Blurb.com

When our clients at the self-publishing site Blurb.com first approached us a few years ago, they didn't have the time or budget for a large UX research project. Yet they needed to understand why some of their customers were abandoning half-created books and what they could do to improve the publishing process. We proposed a single day of remote interviews followed by a directed workshop to generate recommendations, on one condition: their entire core team had to attend the interviews. This meant we were all in the same conference room at Blurb's office with their stakeholders present, but the participant was remote, sharing their screen and audio using GoToMeeting. Prior to that day, we had a couple of one-hour calls with our key contacts, and we presented two short documents for their review.

We did not write a facilitator guide in advance, but instead honed it the day of the interviews, and since we were intercepting people from Blurb.com for the research, half the script was simply just asking them to continue doing what they set out to do on their own. So our live recruiting strategy took care of half the planning process.

The study resulted in several actionable recommendations about both the book-creation tool and how to present it to users, as well as some striking insights into users' mindsets/mental models.

Several key factors made this study work:

- **The entire client team attended.** We weren't doing our interviews in isolation away from the people with the biggest stake in the project, so we had the right group available to approve changes if needed. This meant that we could adjust the interview flow on the fly, even during a session.

- **We didn't write a script, but we did spend our call time getting a solid understanding of the main questions to be answered.** With two experienced interviewers on the project, we had confidence that we could guide an unscripted conversation in such a way that it answered those questions. (And if those had turned out to be the wrong questions based on users' reality, we could have made the shift right away—see previous bullet.)

- **We live-recruited study participants using a Web intercept.** We were confident that participants who answered "What did you come to Blurb.com to do today?" with one of the tasks we were interested in were actually engaged in the task at that moment. Without much direction from us, we'd be able to observe interactions that were important to the study simply by asking them to continue what they had been doing and think aloud.

- **We used an observation and recording method that we had a lot of experience with.** While we ran a solid pre-flight check, we didn't need to do a more extensive proof of concept. We simply used the online meeting tool GoToMeeting to observe users' screens, and Mac screen recording software iShowYouHD to record their screens and phone audio.

- **We managed client expectations.** We made sure our clients knew that findings would emerge from individual (and possibly very differently triggered) behavioral moments that would build into consistent themes. We made everyone promise to ignore the self-reported quotes and focus on behavior. We also didn't provide percentages, severity scales, or other pseudo-quantitative outcomes. With the major players in the room all day, we knew that consensus on observations would be easy.

But why do it this way instead of pushing stakeholders for more time and more preparation? The easy answer is that many organizations truly don't have the time or budget required for full-blown research. We often simply have to work lighter and faster. But there's also a way that a script, in itself, can limit your observations, and so can a strict user profile. When we're working without a script, we're not wedded to a strong presumption of how we'll elicit the answers we need, and when we don't have participants scheduled in advance, we're not wedded to our original idea of the right participant profile. If, after six enlightening interviews, the team feels certain findings are solid and decides to recruit someone from an outlying demographic for extra perspective, that option remains open. Many times, that outside-the-box question or that slightly off user generates the most important finding in a study. One of the reasons we do this is that we hate to miss those times.

by Julie Norvaisas

Julie Norvaisas is a senior researcher at LinkedIn. She was previously a researcher at Portigal Consulting.

The project started innocently enough. At kick-off, our client presented us with a series of hypothesized and storyboard-illustrated consumer needs, along with several early but well thought-out concepts being built to address those needs. Our job was to explore the needs and test the concepts. This seemed straightforward enough, but internal tensions were revealing themselves, even at this meeting.

FIGURE 3.3

Julie Norvaisas, senior researcher at LinkedIn

Some folks on the team were focused on gaining a deeper contextual understanding of the consumer's experience in order to validate and deepen their understanding of their hypothesized consumer needs. This faction had legitimate questions about their hypotheses (which were not based in formal research) and were hungry for insights that could create more texture in their understanding, and inspire further conceptual design. This group was more comfortable with ambiguity in the research and was open to exploratory techniques.

Another group of strong voices was determined to simply gather reactions to the early concepts and prototypes they'd developed. This group had a very high degree of confidence that with their years of experience, they understood the market very well and had already nailed the consumer needs. These people were committed to the concepts and interested in specific feedback to prototypes, down to the level of form factor, mechanical design, materials, interaction, and GUI.

Predictably, the former group was user-experience designers and marketing executives, and the latter was software and hardware engineers and technologists.

Prior to departing for fieldwork in Minnesota, the team needed to ensure that our interview guide met the competing objectives of the stakeholders. We also had to be economical, with only 90 minutes allotted for each interview.

To build consensus, the team met in the only room that happened to be available, a vacant office. We gathered our chairs in a circle in the otherwise empty room. It felt much more like a group therapy session than a meeting!

Rather than painstakingly reviewing the interview guide, we asked everyone to speak about how they felt about it. What were they most excited about? Nervous about? What questions did they still have? What aspects of the interview guide made them feel uncertain? What would make them feel better? We went around in a circle, and we shared. We listened. We acknowledged concerns and addressed them. We mirrored. We prodded.

The be-sure-to-get-us-context folks needed to know that we were going to gain some meaningful understanding of users while asking such specific, granular questions about the concepts. They would not be happy unless we were delving into behavior and motivations, even while talking about the size of a screen. The test-our-concepts faction required assurances that the early getting-to-know-you portion of the interview would not serve as a distraction from critical time spent on the concepts. They stated strongly that we were absolutely not to waste time asking questions regarding needs and usage that they already knew the answers to.

The therapeutic approach worked wonders to surface and resolve what seemed like a real impasse. In the end, everyone felt heard, and together we calibrated the priorities for the interviews. Inclusive conversation established a level of comfort on the team and a shared understanding of our objectives.

Of course, as is so often delightfully the case, our careful intentions were blown up in the first interview. Our first participant told stories that touched the team deeply and immediately had us rethinking the needs and the concept, in the context of her reality. This effect built through subsequent interviews, ultimately changing the thinking of all of the members of the team. The prototypes served more as props to foster discussion about visions of the future than actual artifacts to be evaluated.

In the end, the concept-oriented members led the team to broaden their perception of needs and possible solutions. Original concepts were abandoned. The more reluctant group became the most vocal advocates for a new direction. The fact that all parties were heard and acknowledged prior to the fieldwork created trust despite concerns, and allowed us to be open to what was revealed in the field.

Finding Participants (aka Recruiting)

Finding participants is a crucial part of preparing for fieldwork, yet some teams treat it very casually, relying on friends and family (an approach that is sometimes justified with the "guerilla" rhetoric) or even worse, grabbing barely-screened participants on the street or in a store (this is known as an "intercept"). On the other hand, some UX teams (such as those at Intuit and Salesforce.com) have a full-time staff member whose key responsibility is to manage recruiting.

The first step (sometimes this takes place early on, as you are scoping a project) is to identify the key characteristics for your sample. For example:

- Six active users of blogging software (WordPress, LiveJournal, Blogger, or MovableType) in Chicago, Lisbon, and Tel Aviv

  Two have been blogging for two years or more

  Two have been using their current platform for less than a year

  All between ages of 25 and 55

- Two active blog readers with more than 100 feed subscriptions

A few things to note in this example:

- We're looking at several parts of a transaction (in this case, blog writers and blog readers); even if we are designing only one part of the experience, we can gain a deeper understanding by looking at it from multiple points of view.

- We have a mix of the specific (the list of blogging platforms) and the descriptive. (We don't know yet what makes someone an "active" blogger or reader.)

- Criteria are based more on behavior ("active," "more than 100") than attitude ("dramatic storytellers").

As with the research goals, these criteria should be shared with the project team and iterated so that all parties are on the same page. Also, aligning on these criteria can require "group therapy" (see Julie's "Group Therapy" sidebar). When teams ask themselves who their customers are (or could be), this question surfaces any number of disconnects: hypotheses masquerading as facts, aspirations, and mass hallucinations. You should resolve those issues as tactfully as possible.

For example, in a study that focused on online shopping for athletic apparel, we spent four weeks (of what was supposed to be a six-week project) actively negotiating, among an ever-increasing set of stakeholders, the basic archetypes of customers to look at. It was daunting, but essential for having any success further down the road. We were not able to change the underlying cultural issues that were causing this issue (nor were we trying to), but we were able to use our expertise in planning and executing these sorts of studies to help resolve the deadlock. Although these four weeks were exhausting and frustrating, we did get the team unstuck and moving forward on the research itself.

NOTE RECRUITING IS DATA

> Recruiting draws heavily on the project management skill set, but keep your researcher's eye open for surprises. If it's very challenging to find the people that you expect (or are expected) to do research with, *that's data*. In one project, the fact that I couldn't find anyone with a luxurious yet functional "smart home" implementation revealed a great deal about how that client was conceiving of the market.[1]

From the criteria, I produced a document called a *screener* (see Figure 3.4). This is much like a survey that is used to qualify potential participants. It includes a mix of question types (including yes/no, multiple choice, and open-ended), and uses responses to direct the flow through the set of questions.

Once you have a finalized screener, you have to find participants. There are many approaches, depending on whom you are trying to find. Some organizations have existing customer lists they can pull from (especially for consumers). Others firms may go to their sales staff or other well-connected people for introductions. For consumer research, I almost always use an external market research recruiting agency. They will use our screener and either their own database or customer lists provided by our clients.

This is a time-consuming process; it always takes a week or more to align on the recruiting criteria and the finalized screener (on one project, it took us about four weeks!); a specialized recruiting agency will need about two weeks to recruit participants.

For more on recruiting, check out Chapter 3 of Bolt/Tulathimutte's book called *Remote Research*. Although their context is different (they are recruiting, well, remote participants, and we're recruiting face-to-face participants), the general principles certainly apply here.

---

1 For more on the power of surprises throughout the research process, check out "What to Expect When You're Not Expecting It" by Steve Portigal & Julie Norvaisas, *interactions* March + April 2011 at http://rfld.me/QYGII8.

Portigal Consulting www.portigal.com

2. Do you own a portable MP3 player that you use regularly?

Yes
No **DISMISS**

2a.. If yes, how long have you owned a portable MP3 player?
Less than 3 months **DISMISS**
Between 3 months and 1 year
More than 1 year

2b. If yes, how many hours per week do you estimate you use your portable MP3 player?
IF < 5 THEN DISMISS

3. Do you listen to music on a computer?
Yes
No **DISMISS**

3a. If yes, how often?

Daily
Weekly
Every other week **DISMISS**
Monthly **DISMISS**
Less than once per month **DISMISS**

4. Do you regularly listen to music on any other devices?
Yes (describe______________________)
No

5. How many music CDs do you own? These can be CDs that were purchased or received as gifts. Do not count tracks or albums burned onto CDs.
IF < 60 THEN DISMISS

6. Approximately how many CDs would you estimate you have ripped? (Ripping is the process of copying the audio data from a CD to hard disk)
IF < 20 THEN DISMISS

7. What retail stores do you typically go to when making music CD purchases? Select all that apply.

Circuit City
Best Buy
Good Guys
Wal-Mart

Portigal Consulting: Sample Screener

FIGURE 3.4
One page from a screener.[2]

2 See the complete document at http://rfld.me/VGiHqm.

For participant recruiting, I typically use full-service market research agencies that have their own focus group facilities. (Although you won't be using those facilities in these studies, their presence is a good indicator.) My best experiences are with agencies that I can work with closely through the process. At the outset, they give the screener a close reading, identify missing elements, and verify what isn't clear. As the recruiting process proceeds, they give daily updates (even when they haven't found anyone), and they point out any criteria that are commonly eliminating otherwise good participants, in case we want to make an adjustment.

Great recruiters will establish an initial rapport with your participants and help them feel comfortable and enthusiastic about the process. They will also support you in creating a comfortable schedule, allowing for driving time and rush-hour traffic. Costs for recruiting will vary, based on the complexity and the difficulty of the assignment, but for U.S. consumers, you can expect to pay the recruiter between $150 and $225 each. Note that this is their fee for finding and scheduling the participant and is separate from the incentive you pay to the participant (more on that later).

Creating the Field Guide

The field guide (sometimes called an *interview guide* or more formally, a *protocol*) is a document that details what will happen in the interview (see Figure 3.5). Creating this detailed plan is an essential preparatory step. The interviews themselves never happen as you imagine, but having a detailed plan prepares you to be flexible. It also creates alignment among the team (as do other planning tools). In situations where you have multiple teams of people out in the field, this alignment is essential.

To prepare your field guide, start with your research goals and the other inputs. This is the step where you translate "questions we want answers to" to "questions we will ask." Of course, the guide also covers activities, tasks, logistics, and more.

The general flow of most interview guides is:

- Introduction and participant background
- The main body
- Projection/dream questions
- Wrap up

Portigal Consulting LLC
415.894.2001
2311 Palmetto Avenue Suite D1
Pacifica, CA 94044

www.portigal.com

Reading Ahead Interview Guide

Introduction

1. We'd like to talk with you today about reading. We have lots of questions to ask you, and we're interested in hearing your stories and experiences.

Overview

2. Can you tell us a little about yourself—what you do, hobbies, etc.?

3. Can you tell me about a recent book you've read? Your favorite all-time book?

4. Why do you read?

5. What is your current reading like?
   [Probe for different types of reading, locations, motivations,etc.]

6. Is your current reading typical for you? How so/how is it different?

7. Do you call yourself a "reader?" What does that mean to you?
   [Look for their categories: could be frequency, importance, etc.]

   If you were telling a new acquaintance about yourself, would you talk about reading? What else would you say about yourself?

Exploring Specifics (locations, subject matter, motivations, etc.)

8. You mentioned (<u>follow up on specifics from overview</u>). Is this always the same, or does it change? Why do you do it this way?

9. Have there been any special circumstances where you've done it differently? Why? How was that?

10. Has anything about the way you do this changed over time? How? Why?

Environment

11. What makes a good reading environment for you? What are the elements? What makes an environment not good?

FIGURE 3.5
One page from a field guide.[3]

---

3   A complete example is at http://rfld.me/QBeotb.

Be sure to assign durations to the different sections and subsections. Again, you aren't necessarily going to stick to the exact duration in the actual interview, but it helps you see if you've got enough time to cover everything you are expecting to cover. I prefer to write most questions as I might ask them ("Is there a single word that captures the thing you most like about wine?"), rather than as abstracted topics ("A single word that represents what they like about wine?"). As I'm writing the field guide, I'm leading a mock interview in my head. Using more detailed, thought-out questions helps me put together a more realistic plan.

Introduction and Participant Background

In the introduction, you'll spend just a few minutes getting the interview under way, handling some logistics, and setting expectations. This section of the interview guide might contain the following (italicized text indicates instructions to the interviewer):

- *Give out release form and get signature*

- *Turn on video camera*

- *Confirm timing: 90 minutes*

- *Explain who we are and why we are doing this*

- *There are no wrong answers; this is information that helps us direct our work*

- Tell us about your family. Who lives in this house? How long have you lived here?

The discussion of participant background serves as an icebreaker and also provides some context for later in the interview.

The Main Body

As the name suggests, this is the bulk of the interview guide (and the interview). You should create subsections for each of the areas you want to explore (such as configuration, learning about features, downloading new playlists). The main body should also include the exercises and activities that you plan to use (such as mapping, card sorting, demonstrations, and reactions to prototypes or other stimuli).

For a study seeking feedback about a prototype home entertainment device, our main body topics were:

- Revisit concepts
- Map your technology
- Context of use
- Concept discussion

Be deliberate in how you sequence these sections. You can start with the general and then dive into specifics; you can start with present day and move backward; you can start with a previous time and move toward the current state. There's no universal rule here, so much depends on your topic and how you are mentally picturing the inquiry. Remember the participant may take things in a different direction, so don't sweat too much over this. It's easy to revise the overall flow once you've completed a couple of the interviews.

Projection/Dream Questions

Near the end of the interview is a great opportunity to ask more audacious questions. Because you've spent all this time with your participants, talking through a topic in detail, they've become engaged with you. You've earned their permission to ask them to go even farther beyond the familiar. Two questions that work really well here are:

- If we came back in five years to have this conversation again, what would be different?

- If you could build your ideal experience, what would it be like?

Wrap Up

A typical interview guide concludes with some basic questions and instructions:

- Did we miss anything? Is there anything you want to tell us?

- Is there anything you want to ask us?

- *Thank then and give the incentive.*

Shot List

As an appendix to the field guide, list the photos you want to capture (see Figure 3.6), such as the following:

- Head shot of participant

- Participant and key piece of equipment

- Close-up of key piece of equipment

- Establishing shots, interior (cubicle or living room) and exterior

- Two-shot of interviewer and participant

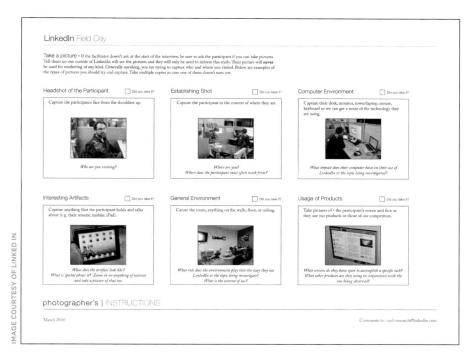

FIGURE 3.6
A visual shot list created by researchers at LinkedIn.

As with the other preparation tools, share the field guide with your team. The typical audience for the field guide tends to be broader than for the more tactical tools like a screener. I also try to help the people reviewing it understand what the field guide is (and what it isn't) so that they can effectively help it evolve. I've used the following in an explanatory email:

> Remember, this is not a script. It reads very linearly, but it's really just a tool to prepare to be flexible. Questions don't get asked in the order they're written here, or using this exact language (so it doesn't need to be proofread). If you could look at it with an eye toward calling out anything that we haven't covered—e.g., "We need to ask about how they deal with time zones"—or any larger topic areas that are missing, or anything that seems wildly off base, that would be the most helpful.

Scheduling Interviews

If you are interviewing professionals about their work, you may need to run your interviews during (or just before/after) their work hours. If you are interviewing consumers, you may have to conduct interviews in the evening or on weekends. In the latter case, it can be helpful to set that expectation early on with colleagues who will be participating. Remind them that you're trying to embrace the participant's worldview, and they can begin that process by adapting their schedule and availability to the participant's lifestyle, not the opposite.

When scheduling your fieldwork days, don't be too ambitious. Although focus group and usability moderators tend to set up camp in a facility and run sessions back to back for a full day or more, I think that's generally a terrible idea and especially when doing fieldwork. Quality work doesn't come from being rushed, exhausted, harried, or overwhelmed. Interviewing is hard work. You need time between sessions to reflect on what you learned, adjust your approach for the next interview, get to the next interview location, find food, and find a bathroom. Although this becomes more dramatic when you are driving around a metropolitan area interviewing people in their homes, it's still true, even when moving around a corporate facility during a site visit.

Leave time in between your interviews. Don't pack too many into a day. Depending on the constraints (Are you on-site? Are you on the road? How long are the interviews?), two interviews a day is reasonable. The schedule is at least partly informed by participant availability, so you may end up with an early morning interview, several hours of free time, and then an evening interview on one day, and then two back-to-back interviews the next day. That's fine. Just don't try to do several days in a row with too many interviews.

Travel

The same sanity clause applies to travel situations: if you're travelling locally, try to schedule your interviews so they are close together geographically. If you're working with recruiters, they should take care of this. If you're travelling on a plane, allow time for your plane to be late before your first interview, and avoid having an interview that will run into your head-to-the-airport window, because that will destroy your ability to be present in the interview. Even better, keep travel days and interview days separate. If you are travelling internationally, leave yourself at least a day to adjust to the time zone differences, and to soak up the local culture, before you dive into fieldwork.

Participant Releases and Non-Disclosure Agreements

A *release* is a good idea. A release is a document that you have your interviewee sign. It clarifies the rights that the interviewee and the interviewer (and their organization) have. The text of the release may address a number of issues:

- **Consent:** Being in the study is voluntary, and the participant can stop at any time.

- **Incentive:** The amount of money that will be given, and that the exchange of money doesn't mean that the participant is an employee.

- **Model release:** Images and video will be used without giving the participant any rights of approval.

- **Non-disclosure:** The participant is obligated not to reveal anything about concepts he may see.

Although there are ethical reasons to use a release, it's really a legal document. If your organization has a legal department, they will likely want to create this document for you. You should work with them to strike the right balance between legally efficacious terminology and regular-folks lingo.

In situations where you are not revealing any concepts of artifacts that might be considered confidential, you may want to streamline the release by eliminating the non-disclosure agreement (or NDA).

> **NOTE** RELEASE ME
>
> This is the point in the book where I was going to include a best-in-class example of a release. In the time I spent writing this book, I corresponded with researchers at many different corporations and consultancies. Plenty of them are saddled with a legalese-intense release. For those who had managed to wrangle something more palatable to their participants, I was not able to get access to those documents for inclusion here. My colleagues were all very helpful, but when it came down to it, they couldn't get permission to share their release forms.
>
> Now think about this—it's a document that is given out to members of the public (research participants). As I stated earlier in this chapter, even the recruiting process gives you data, especially when it doesn't turn out as you expected. To me, this highlights the (appropriate, necessary) risk aversion

that characterizes a corporate legal department. While sharing best practices or being identified as a thought leader may be appealing to a researcher at a leading corporation, that has less importance than even the remote possibility of legal exposure. For you, as you craft a release that satisfies the needs of these different audiences, be aware of where values intersect and where they don't. Good luck!

If you work for an agency conducting this research on behalf of a client, the release may be an agreement between your organization and the participant, enabling you to keep the study "blind" (which means the participant does not know the name of the sponsoring organization), which is usually preferable. However, if you work for an agency and your client is asking for non-disclosure, you will probably want to use the client's NDA and have that particular aspect of the agreement be between the participant and the client directly.

Incentives

The right incentive amount depends on where you are doing research and what you are asking of the participant. If you are using a recruiting agency, they can advise you on a recommended incentive. Think of the incentive not as compensation but as an enthusiastically demonstrative thank you. In professional situations (interviewing people at their workplace), a monetary incentive given directly to the participant may not be appropriate. It may be prohibited by the participant's employer, it may be unethical or at least awkward if your participant is a customer, and if you are interviewing individuals within a group (say an emergency room) on an ad hoc basis, it may be less clear who to incentivize and at what proportion. In those cases, look for alternatives.

> **NOTE** BE CREATIVE ABOUT INCENTIVES
>
> You want a simple and direct way to demonstrate your enthusiasm and appreciation. When interviewing credit-default swap traders in London's financial district, my client escort would stop en route at a Starbucks and load up with Venti drinks and baked goods. Even though we had scheduled appointments, our appearance on the trading floor was a small celebration. We've brought pizza into hospitals when interviewing respiratory techs and made charitable donations on behalf of PR firms.

by Harry Boadwee

Harry Boadwee is the founder of the Boadwee Law Office in Cupertino, California. He focuses on technology transactions, software, and Internet law.

Participant agreements for user research are simple but necessary in order to protect the study sponsors. Although a contract can be formed by spoken promises or by a loose exchange of emails, the best and most common practice is to sign a contract. Participant agreements must be short, often no longer than a page, so that participants can read and sign them quickly, without negotiation. Even a document with a short-form title, such as "Permission" or "Release," can be a contract.

A typical participant agreement covers two main concerns:

- First, the participant agrees to keep confidential the information disclosed in the study and make no use of the information beyond participation in the study. Such information can include, for example, the questions raised in the study, as well as the details of the product or service being studied. For example, many studies cover early-stage concepts or unreleased products/services. Study sponsors obviously don't want participants to disclose this information to competitors or (even worse) to the public by blogging or tweeting about it.

- Second, the participant will grant permission to the sponsor to record, reproduce, display, and distribute the participant's responses, voice, and likeness without any additional compensation or royalty. A "likeness" can encompass video, photographs, or even drawings. The study may include some small consideration, such as a T-shirt or gift card for a token amount. The release is needed in order to prevent legal claims for compensation under the privacy and publicity laws of many states. These releases often include an explicit waiver of any right to inspect or approve the materials created in the study.

These types of releases most often cover the sponsor's internal use only. Because the concepts and products/services in the study often are in an early stage, the sponsor probably wouldn't want to use a participant's statements as a public testimonial. If it did, the sponsor would need to obtain a separate testimonial release permitting public display and distribution of the participant's responses, voice, and likeness, and if desired, the participant's name and address.

Similarly, if the study sponsor wants detailed testing and feedback concerning a product as used by numerous participants in their homes or offices, the sponsor would use a "beta evaluation agreement" instead.

Participants less than 18 years old generally do not have the legal right in most states to form a contract. Instead, a parent or legal guardian should enter into the contract on their behalf. Participant agreements and the issues that they cover are governed by state law, which might create different or additional requirements depending on the state.

You can have your recruiting agency deal with the incentives. For a handling fee, they will mail out checks to your participants after interviews are completed (although you should follow up with them to make sure they act promptly). However, to convey my enthusiastic appreciation, I really prefer the immediate gratification of an envelope of cash handed over as the interview concludes. Obviously, think carefully about how much cash you are carrying and in what situations. Either way, make sure that your participants know ahead of time when they'll be getting their incentive.

If you deliver the incentive yourself, you can go beyond a plain envelope and include a thank-you note as well. Field researchers from a large financial institution, cognizant that participants are also customers, supplement their incentives with logo-emblazoned goodies (a reusable grocery bag containing an aluminum water bottle and a reusable lunch bag).

Summary

It takes a lot of preparation—perhaps a surprising amount—to set up successful field research. I don't recommend leaping into the field-work without setting yourself up to be successful. The effort in creating alignment, developing a plan, and determining the logistics pays off tremendously in the quality of the experience for you, stakeholders, and participants and in the value of the insights gathered.

- Agreeing to the objectives for field research is crucial, but is often challenging. You may all agree that you are going to interview 12 typical users before you are able to agree on what you expect to learn and how that will inform your business.

- Use the documents you create in planning (research goals, screener, and interview guide) to align with your team.

- Consider broadly and choose specifically what types of partici-pants you want. But treat this as a hypothesis and adjust your approach if necessary.

- Leave time in your project plan to find research participants.

- The field guide is the detailed plan of what you think might happen in the interview, typically flowing from the details to their mean-ing. Having that detailed plan empowers you to be flexible when you actually go into the field.

- When scheduling interviews, leave adequate time between them for reflection, eating, travel, and the bathroom. Don't overload your day—and your poor brain—with too many interviews.

- Use a release that documents the rights and obligations of both the organization that sponsors the research and the participant.

- Give participants an incentive that conveys your sincere apprecia-tion of their time.

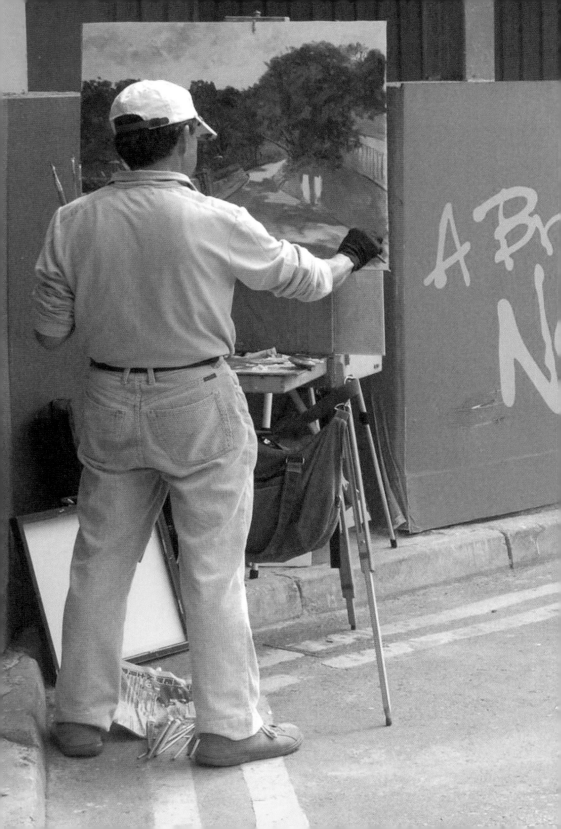

More Than Just Asking Questions

Although the title of this book emphasizes *interviewing*, when you get down to it, *interviewing* involves more than just *interviewing*. Did I just blow your mind? I bet that I did. But dust yourself off, acknowledge the glory of recursion, and let's move on! Interviewing is absolutely the core of the interaction with your participant, but there are other techniques (or if you prefer, *methods*; or if you really prefer, *methodologies*). You should consider the interview itself as a platform and try to organically integrate a larger set of techniques.

Showing and Telling

Even when your only technique is asking questions, there are many ways to get to the information you are seeking. I'll go further into the types of questions in Chapter 6, "How to Ask Questions." The phrasing of the question itself leads to a variety of techniques. If one of your research objectives is to understand how people are managing their digital music, you might ask your participants specifically, "What is your process for updating your playlists?" With that question, the participant is being asked to verbally summarize a (potentially detailed) behavior, from memory. This isn't necessarily a bad approach; it may be interesting to hear which steps in the process are memorable and which ones aren't. It's also a chance to get some emotional color. ("Oh, it's easy, all I do is....") But it's not going to be the most accurate information. By asking, "What is your process for updating your playlists?" we are actually learning the answers to the (unasked) "How do you feel about the process for updating playlists?" and "What are the key steps you can recall in the process for updating playlists?" That information is very important, but it may not be sufficient to really understand the user's situation.

Now, a slightly different expression of the question is "Can you show me how you update your playlists?" Now you've staged an activity. In this activity, you and your participant will move to where the relevant devices are, and you will be able to observe the specific steps in completing this task. Of course, you're also going to gather the emotional context of the process. I sat with a financial advisor who struggled to navigate his intranet in order to find some critical data. His lack of success in locating this data was so frustrating that he began to laugh. Of course, it wasn't comical per se, but he felt that the failures of the system were absolutely ludicrous, and the laughter clearly revealed his perspective.

Although a topic such as playlist updating may be specific to that participant's personal devices and data, in situations where the process is more general, you may try a slight variation, shifting to a participant-observation dialogue, such as, "Can you show me how I should prepare coffee?" Instead of the subject going through her own process, narrating the different steps as *she* would perform them, your question directs her to explain specifically each step so that *you* can perform it, such as, "Now, before you put the filter in, make sure the water is boiling." Asking that person to play the teacher role not only reinforces the idea that she is the expert here, but it also can make it easier for her to articulate the details you are seeking.

> **NOTE** PARTICIPANT OBSERVATION
>
> Participant observation doesn't mean observation of the participant; it means that you observe by participating. I'm typically using the term *participant* to refer to the research subject, but in this approach, you are the participant because you are participating in the activities you are seeking to understand.

Depending on the activity, you may arrange to be present when it occurs. I once sat in a family's kitchen at 7:00 A.M. and watched as they went through their morning food prep rituals. (Yes, that was very early. The only thing worse than the feeling of getting up so early to do fieldwork was the look on our participants' faces when they opened the door to let me in. Sure, they agreed to it ahead of time, but I was certainly not their favorite person at that particular moment.) I didn't need to ask them to show me how coffee was prepared because I knew ahead of time that this was when coffee was going to be prepared. In addition to seeing the operation of the coffee machine, I saw a great deal of context—what other devices were being used, who else was around, what happened before, and what happened after.

You can also work with your participant to stage the activity you want to understand. Although you can expect that breakfast will be eaten most days, you can't be sure that the IT department will be installing a new router every day. However, if you bring them a router when you come for your interview, you've created the occasion.

Another approach more suited for unpacking interactions between people is role-playing how this interaction does (or should) take place. In a project where we looked at customer service experiences, a man complained emphatically but without specificity about the phone service at his local department store. I asked him what he objected to, or how it could be different, but he struggled to find anything to tell me beyond his general dissatisfaction with the way things were. Instead, I suggested that he act as the person answering the phone, and I would act as him, and he could show me how it should work. After describing the exercise, I held an imaginary phone to my head and said "Ring, ring!" (see Figure 4.1). He answered his imaginary phone, and we proceeded to model the ideal conversation. Afterward, we talked about how our version differed from his typical experience.

FIGURE 4.1
Shifting the discussion from the conceptual to the tangible (even when being tangible means being fantastical) is one way to get at hard-to-uncover information.

Participatory design, a term that sometimes refers to an overall approach to design, is essentially giving people the tools to show us how they envision a new design or solution. This can take many forms: I've created blank versions of a mobile device screen and had participants draw the UI, and I've seized the moment when participants starting envisioning a new solution and helped them to grab whatever was nearby. (One participant grabbed a hard cover book as a proxy for size and form factor, but then proceeded to gesture with the book as if it really were this future device.) Designers sometimes get nervous with participatory design because it implies that users will tell them what to design, and they'll be expected to go off and implement it. Of course, that's not true at all. Participants may decide their ideal product needs a handle. But we know that really means that they need an easy way to move it from place to place, and we know that there are dozens of ways to satisfy that need. My aim with participatory design is to give people a different way to talk about needs, where the solutions stand as proxies for those needs.

No one of these interrelated techniques is inherently better than the others. Any of them may be appropriate, depending on what you want to know, what you've already asked, and what is working well between you and your participant. You may also want to combine these approaches to look for points of divergence. For example, if you observe a certain coffee preparation step that is excluded from the process your participant teaches you, that's something you can ask about: "I noticed that when you were making coffee earlier you waited until the water boiled before you put the filter in. That wasn't something you told me to do. Is it an important part of the process?" As with so many aspects of the work you're doing, you want to have a broad palette of approaches that you can bring to bear as circumstances warrant.

Bring the Tools

This section explains a set of techniques that involves using prepared physical materials to facilitate the interview, including maps, various forms of representing concepts, organizing and sorting artifacts, and "provocative" images.

Mapping

A map is a tangible representation that shifts the abstract (such as a process, a set of relationships, or the details of a large physical space) into a concrete artifact. This artifact provides a focal point for more detailed discussions and is documentation that can be taken with you at the end of the interview. In one example, architects and designers mapped out their fairly complex workflow (indicating software packages, file formats, processes, contributors, output, and so on) using sticky notes (where each color represented a certain class of element) on a large piece of butcher paper. In a project for Nokia Research Center that involved exploring the notion of convergence, tech-savvy consumers drew a map of their homes and indicated where their technology was located and how it was connected together (see Figure 4.2). The interviewer facilitated the process of drawing the map by probing and prompting. As the map was built, both the participant and the interviewer developed a shared understanding. As the interview proceeded, the interviewer could continually refer to the information on the map—for example, by pointing to an element and clarifying "So that would be when you're over here, then?" The map became a crucial element in the analysis and synthesis work after the fieldwork was over, as the interviewer used it to relate pertinent details to his colleagues.

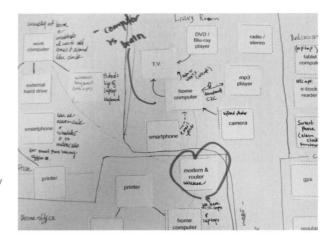

FIGURE 4.2
A participant's hand-drawn map shows how technology was connected together in his home.

Reactions to Concepts

I don't like to call this "concept testing" because that implies the key to the approach is to present a solution and have participants evaluate it. What you present need not represent an actual solution. For example, you often show concepts that are not viable or otherwise unlikely in order to explore the edges of factors that influence desirability, usefulness, and so on (see Figure 4.3). What you're learning is not an evaluation of the concept, but instead a deeper understanding of the design criteria for a future solution. Although concepts are the stimuli, you deliberately choose stimuli that contain some aspect of your hypotheses, ideas, or questions in a tangible form.

FIGURE 4.3
Although you wouldn't develop a mobile phone this tiny, you could provoke an interesting dialogue by showing it to someone. It would be much harder to have a discussion about button size, screen size, ear-canal risk, and so on, if you only had a set of "best" solutions on hand.

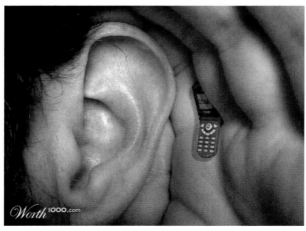

WORTH1000.COM AND ROBERTO (HTTP://ALL.WORTH1000.COM/ARTISTS/ROBERTO)

NOTE GO INDIRECTLY

As with participatory design, solutions that you show can stand as proxies for something else. You aren't asking questions about their *needs* (say, their expectations for a device's size), but rather you are asking questions about a *concept* in order to elicit, among other feedback, their expectations for the device's size. This can be quite indirect; the stimuli don't actually reveal to the participant what it is that you want to know, what is feasible, what is planned, or what your hypotheses are. There's a difference between what you want to know and what you ask. Let yourself be creative when developing these provocative stimuli.

I'll go to the interview with a set of specific topics I'm looking for feedback about, but it's important to let the participants structure most of the response themselves. I'll put the concept in front of them, with whatever explanation or demonstration I've planned, and then ask them an open-ended question such as "What do you think?" The topics they choose themselves are the strongest natural reactions. If they start off raving about the keyboard but don't mention the screen until I ask about it, that's an important takeaway. It's my job to make sure I hear about the keyboard, the screen, and all the other topics of interest, but the concerns and delights that they express unprompted are critical.

One caution here: depending on your individual role, you may feel a certain amount of ownership of the concept. But as I urged you in Chapter 2, "A Framework for Interviewing," you should have checked your worldview at the door and be ready to embrace how someone else sees the world. You should present your concepts neutrally in order to give the participants as much freedom in their responses as possible. Even if you begin your interview with "We're here to get your feedback, so don't worry about hurting our feelings," if you bring out a concept by saying, "Here's something I've been working on…" you're activating a natural social instinct that will diminish their comfort in being critical. The disclaimer at the beginning works at a different (and less effective) level than the cues you give off in the way you present concepts. Before you go into the field, practice "the reveal" aloud until you hear yourself sounding neutral (try "Here's a whole bunch of early ideas that I was asked to show you" or "I'll be curious to hear what you think of this one" or "Our clients are exploring some possible ideas"). I've often found the concepts themselves are sufficiently complex (because of the technology that's being used or the domain of work that is being supported) that I'm not able to present them effectively. In that case, my client will handle that part of the interview: I'll introduce the exercise (with the neutral language), my client will give a neutral demonstration of the concept, and I will ask the first open-ended question.

One more caution here: If participants perceive you as having ownership over the concept, they may turn the interview back on you: "Will this be backward-compatible?" "How much will it cost?" "Does it have high fructose corn syrup in the sauce?" Do not answer those questions. This is a terrible struggle for my clients who always have the answers and would feel so much more comfortable in the familiar scenario where they are the experts about this topic. Once again, do not answer those questions. Do the *Interviewer Sidestep* and turn the question back to them: "Is that important to you?" "What would you expect it to be?"

Concept Formats

There is no limit to the manner of concepts you can develop for researching with users. But it's important to realize that you are creating these concepts for that very purpose: showing to users. You've probably seen shiny prototypes that are intended to get investors, retailers, or managers excited. But I urge clients to represent their ideas in lower, rather than higher, fidelity[1]. As a rule of thumb, lower-fidelity prototypes are best for getting reactions earlier in the process (when you are trying to understand the appeal of the idea), and higher-fidelity prototypes are better for later in the process (when you want to verify some specific aspect of the implementation). There are always exceptions. If you are presenting a futuristic concept, you may want to be very high fidelity in your representation in order to get participants past the inevitable "Well, what would that actually be like?" questions and into the area you want to explore.

High fidelity is not an all-encompassing term. There are different dimensions of fidelity—for example, "looks like" versus "works like." A prototype that simulates an experience may be high fidelity along one dimension but not another. Align your concept representation with your research question.

Here are a few formats for presenting concepts:

- **Storyboard:** An illustration, typically across multiple panels, depicting a scenario. I used storyboards (see Figure 4.4) when working with MediaMaster, a digital music start-up that was trying to choose among a number of different directions in their product development.

- **Physical mock-up:** A representation of a physical product that can be touched, opened, and so on. The team at Nokia Research Center mocked up a number of size variations on a mobile device using foam core and a printout of a screen design (see Figure 4.5, left). Tursiogear, a start-up company, provided an early manufacturing prototype of an iPod video case that I showed to consumers in order to help understand the features they were expecting (see Figure 4.5, right).

---

1   For an engaging and helpful read, see Houde/Hill's classic "What Do Prototypes Prototype?" http://rfld.me/Wnig5s

Step 2

At checkout, Associate scans barcode on front of envelope. Upon purchase, envelope is "activated".

Step 3

When Megan gets home, she follows directions on the envelope and takes the CD booklets out of her CD cases. She counts the booklets, puts them in the envelope.

Step 4

Megan goes online to complete the purchase, selects file formats, and signs-up for a free account. She then drops the envelope in the mail.

FIGURE 4.4
Detail of one of several storyboards showing the different scenarios that MediaMaster was considering developing.

FIGURE 4.5
Physical mock-ups from Nokia (left) and Tursiogear (right) help make the conversation about a future product tangible.

I've even used this physical mock-up approach for non-technology projects. When studying how people reacted to different messages in a gas company's credit card newsletter, I used fairly realistic examples of this newsletter, complete with a sample credit card statement and their official envelope. Although most of the newsletter was actual English, the back page had a number of articles with "Greeked" text (lorem ipsum, and so on). One participant noticed this text and (thinking that it was Spanish) commented that the inclusion of a second language was a great idea! It was a good reminder that our assumptions about elements in a concept are often shattered in the field. In a slightly more challenging situation, I arrived at the research session to find that my client, who was not Apple, had echoed (to put it charitably) the iPhone form factor in a solid model mock-up for a hand-held device. (Their logic was that they were going to try to mock it up later using an iPhone, so....) Every participant therefore assumed that the product would be made by Apple (it wasn't), and that it would be usable not only around the home but also could be taken out and used away from the home (it wouldn't). I had to adjust for those influencing factors in interpreting the results of the sessions.

- **Wireframe:** A simplified version of an on-screen interface. This could be printed, sketched on paper, or a combination. It could be presented on a screen (say, a laptop or tablet). It could be a series of screens that depict a flow with real or simulated interactivity. We showed currency traders a data-free mock-up of their trading platform to uncover which elements had to be carried forward into a redesign and which elements they were receptive to seeing changed. In the previously mentioned Nokia Research Center project, their team produced an iPad-based simulation of a mobile device UI (see Figure 4.6) that we used in combination with a physical mock-up (see Figure 4.5, left).

FIGURE 4.6
Nokia used an iPad to demonstrate the on-screen interaction for a future product concept.

NOTE IMPROVISING WITH A WOUNDED PROTOTYPE

Working with Hewlett-Packard on research for their DVD/ digital projector, I met up with my client at the Denver airport a few hours before we were to head out for our first interview. He was traveling with an *engineering breadboard,* which is a working model cobbled together from parts and controls and stuffed into an electronics case. (This is a "works like" but not a "looks like.") Too big to carry on, it came as checked baggage. Oops. While it was physically intact, my client quickly realized that the audio no longer worked. In our scant time, we scrambled to borrow multi-tools and other weapons of engineering destruction. The back seat of our rental car became a mobile bench as he struggled in vain to repair it before fieldwork commenced. In the end, it was fine, even without sound. We showed participants how the device played a DVD and projected the image on their walls. And then we asked them to describe the qualities of the audio they would expect in order to match the video experience the prototype delivered. For more about this project, see **www.portigal.com/wp/wp-content/ uploads/2006/03/Steve-Portigal-DUX05-Projective-Techniques-for-Projection-Technologies.pdf**.

Reactions to Other Stuff

Other stimuli can be helpful in probing people's underlying belief structures, expectations, or motivations. As with the mapping tools, these stimuli are an interactive and tangible way to help people express themselves. And as before, there are endless ways to provoke participants. Here are just a couple:

- **Casual card sort:** In contrast to the more rigorous card-sorting process that is used in software design[2], this is a way to prompt a discussion about a large set of items. For one project, I used cards that depicted a large set of online services (see Figure 4.7). For another project, the cards illustrated many items that people purchased on a regular basis. As the cards were spread out, people began to talk about those that were relevant to them, prompting stories or highlighting areas for follow-up questions. Some groupings may emerge with this process, and the cards can be used as a tool for confirming your understanding of the participant's mental model, as in "So it sounds like these two cards would go together because you see these as examples of something you do for work, but not for your personal use?" Of course, you can create new cards based on what you hear (bring blank ones!), or you can annotate the cards to reflect what the participant has told you.

---

2   You can find a great primer on traditional card sorting at http://rfld.me/R4c3WG.

FIGURE 4.7
The primary online services that our research participant mentioned, selected from a larger set.

- **Images that resonate:** These images can also be cards, or a printed sheet, or stickers (see Figure 4.8). Whatever the medium, they depict a large number of images that are meant to evoke an emotional reaction. Consider stock photos, glamour shots of products, celebrities, historical images, nature and landscape images, textures, colors, and so on. (A variation might be to include words in the set as well.) With this large set of diverse stimuli, you can ask people to pick a few images that address something you're interested in. In past projects, I've asked people to select images that evoked their ideal online experience with our client's brand, or that represented the way they hoped a new printer could change their lives. The most insightful part happens when you ask participants why they picked those images. They'll tell you—in surprising ways—what it is about those images that speaks to them and how those characteristics represent their hopes, aspirations, or ideal solution.

FIGURE 4.8
Laminated image cards are used to provoke individual reactions and uncover hidden associations.

Homework

Often the thing we are most interested in happens in a series of smaller interactions over a course of days and weeks. In that case, give your participant a homework assignment. When I wanted to understand how people would react to a credit card newsletter, I asked participants to save their postal mail for a few days, without opening it. During our interview, they narrated their mail sorting process, explaining what they would keep and what they would trash. When I then showed our prototype newsletter in its envelope, we had a solid context for investigating the meaning of the newsletter. Similarly, when Beringer was redesigning its Stone Cellars wine packaging, we asked our participants to save a week's worth of empty bottles. Between their unopened wine, the empty bottles, and the sample bottles we brought with us, we had a wide range of example packages to look at together.

I also use homework as a way to prime participants about a topic I'm interested in. In other words, it helps people reach a state where they are more introspective about something they may not pay attention to otherwise. I've asked people to log when they use their mobile phone, take screen shots of every intranet search, or document all their banking activities. This certainly produces all sorts of curious instances, provocative examples, and weak signals about possible behavior patterns, but this self-documentation (sometimes called *journaling* or a *diary study*) really pays off during a follow-up interview. Not only do you have an extensive set of examples to discuss, but you also have a participant who has been thinking about a topic a lot more than she normally does. (You can see this happen during interviews as well; I'll discuss this more in Chapter 5, "Key Stages of the Interview.") That reflection will lead to a better conversation. Of course, a primed user is not in her natural state, so don't prime if your goal is to understand what's already top of mind.

A specific type of priming is used to accelerate the usage of a product. I took a streaming music server to digital music enthusiasts and asked them to install it while I watched. At the end of the interview, I left them with a workbook that contained about two weeks' worth of assignments, asking them to explore a different feature or use case. Given that people would be unlikely to explore a product that thoroughly in two weeks (if ever, especially given the complexity of this particular product), it was crucial to give people a structure—and a motivation—to drive their usage. After two weeks, we collected their workbooks and then returned for a follow-up interview.

Summary

Be creative in developing a range of methods for any one project. While interviewing is at the core, it's really a platform that can organically include a larger set of techniques that goes beyond merely asking questions. For example, you can vary the activities in the session itself, ask participants to prepare for the interview, or take materials specifically to facilitate the discussion. You can also do the following:

- Ask for a demonstration of an activity that might not otherwise take place.

- Observe a behavior or a task as it happens to occur naturally.

- Use a mapping exercise to create a tangible representation of something abstract that you can refer to repeatedly throughout the interview (and then take away with you at the end).

- Show provocative concepts at varying levels of fidelity and create concepts that will generate discussion around the issues at hand (rather than testing your best guess at the best solution).

- Use images as stimuli to prompt a deeper discussion. When mounted on cards, they can be sorted, grouped, annotated, referred to later, and so on.

- Assign homework (for example, take a few pictures, save some artifacts, complete a questionnaire, and document a set of activities) to give you some data before the interview and to prime the participant about the interview topics

CHAPTER 5

Key Stages of the Interview

Most people are at least conversationally familiar with the Kübler-Ross model of the five stages of grief: denial, anger, bargain, depression, and acceptance. This model describes a consistent set of elements in a very human experience. At the same time, Kübler-Ross pointed out that people don't necessarily experience *all* those stages or experience them in that order.

A contrasting model is the *beat sheet* (see Figure 5.1), a tool for screenwriters that lays out the necessary sections of a typical three-act screenplay, a ubiquitous structure for Hollywood films. There are even beat-sheet calculators that will take the number of pages of a screenplay as input and identify on what specific pages the different story elements should appear. While Kübler-Ross is descriptive, beat sheets are predictive. While being predictive might seem a limitation when making movies, this consistent structure and the reliance on other tropes is part of what makes movies work: viewers are being taught the code with every experience.

```
                  THE BLAKE SNYDER BEAT SHEET

     PROJECT TITLE:
     GENRE:
     DATE:

     1. Opening Image (1):

     2. Theme Stated (5):

     3. Set-Up (1-10):

     4. Catalyst (12):

     5. Debate (12-25):

     6. Break into Two (25):

     7. B Story (30):

     8. Fun and Games (30-55):

     9. Midpoint (55):

     10. Bad Guys Close In (55-75):

     11. All Is Lost (75):

     12. Dark Night of the Soul (75-85):

     13. Break into Three (85):

     14. Finale (85-110):

     15. Final Image (110):
```

FIGURE 5.1
The beat sheet outlines a standardized structure for storytelling via a screenplay.

I've identified the stages that most interviews go through, and my model is somewhere between descriptive and predictive. You may notice some or all of these stages in your interviews, but you can't anticipate, for example, that one will (or should!) happen precisely at the 40-minute mark. But each stage requires specific tactical preparation or responses from you, the interviewer. Get familiar with the details of the stages, and if you don't recognize them while reading, you probably will the next time you are out in the field. As you gain experience, moving through these stages will become secondhand.

But Wait! Before You Head Out: Roles for the Field Team

Generally speaking, I find the ideal size for the field team to be two people: one to lead the interview, and one to back up the other person. In some cases, it's important to expose as many people as possible directly to users, so more people join the sessions. From social psychology, we know that even the presence of others will influence behavior, so be cautious. Even three interviewers will shift the power dynamic and make some participants awkward and less open. This is especially true in a home environment and can be exacerbated depending on the age and gender of the people involved. If I'm asked to field a team of three, I make sure that everyone is aware of the trade-off we're making between more team exposure and less open interviews. I'm extremely resistant to anything larger.

A Guide to Participating in Fieldwork

It's crucial that everyone going into the field understands their roles and that the two or three people who are meeting participants will act in concert, performing like a team. Typically, I convene a brief in-person or telephone meeting where all the potential fieldwork attendees come together to review some basic rules. I'm not trying to make instant expert interviewers out of these folks; I'm looking to pass along the minimum information to ensure these interviews are successful. By handing out the following guide and talking through it, I am starting a conversation about expectations and roles.

Here is an example of how I might introduce the guide when I'm talking to my fellow participants:

A Guide to Participating in Fieldwork

Thanks for joining our research team in the field. Your participation in this part of the process will benefit the overall results of our collaboration.

Although fieldwork may appear on the surface to be a straightforward conversation, you will soon see that a lot more is going on. We don't expect you to be an expert interviewer, although you'll find that you get better with practice. Here are a few tips to help you get the most out of your experience and help us work better together:

- One of us (Portigal Consulting) will be the *lead interviewer.* You will be *second interviewer.* (Kind of like "second chair" on *Law and Order,* where this lawyer sits next to the "first chair," actively observing and strategizing without conducting any of the questioning.) The lead interviewer runs the interview. They also coordinate the participation of the second interviewer.

- Stay engaged! Even if you are not asking questions, listen actively. That means thinking about what you are hearing, making eye contact, nodding affirmatively, and taking notes. You aren't just a "fly on the wall"; you are participating.

- Interviews are different from conversation. We'll use a relaxed tone, but we are purposefully guiding the interaction, often thinking several questions ahead. Although you may not see the path the lead interviewer is on, as the second interviewer, it's important not to interject in a way that can interrupt the flow.

- Write down and hold your questions for the appropriate time. Interviews unfold like the chapters of a book. Your questions need to stay within those chapters. It's the job of the lead interviewer to move the interview from one chapter to the next. The lead interviewer will create opportunities—usually at the ends of these chapters—for you to ask questions.

- We aren't the experts. The people we are interviewing are the experts. We want to gather their stories and opinions, and to hear what they have to say without influencing them. Use their language and terminology. If they refer to a product, brand, or feature inaccurately, don't correct them explicitly or implicitly.

- Use open-ended questions. Don't presume what you think the answer should be.

  Less good: *"What are three things you liked about using the bus?"*

  Good: *"Can you tell me about your experience using the bus?"*

  We don't know that they liked anything about their experience on the bus!

---

1 Also available as a PDF at http://rfld.me/PFG8dP.

Everyone Stays Engaged

Another approach I've seen teams take is to assign explicit roles (such as note taker, photographer, videographer, and so on). I am suspicious this is partly busy-work, akin to giving a toddler a complex toy to play with so they don't get distracted during a long car ride; it is beneficial to distribute those tasks, but it's also more well-defined to serve as the *photographer* than the *second interviewer*. My preference is to set someone up as an interviewer and then, when we meet individually before the interview (say, 30 minutes before, at a nearby café), explore that person's comfort and interest with any of the various roles.

One executive asked me hesitantly about joining in the fieldwork, promising that he'd just be there to observe and wouldn't be involved. But this isn't surgery; it's an engagement with another person. I told him that his participation was at least welcome, and at best necessary, but his role would be an active one, even if it was mostly active listening.

There are a number of techniques for managing the second interviewer and his understandably naive impulse to ask whatever question he thinks of at the moment he thinks of it. You can provide him with sticky notes to write his questions on as he thinks of them (so even if the asking is deferred, at least capturing the question provides some—albeit muted—immediate gratification). You can set aside a period of time at the end of the entire interview for his questions (although this may be asking him to "hold it" for a long period of time, and you may observe some squirming; further, the questions are perhaps decreasingly relevant as the interview proceeds). You can set aside a time for him to ask questions within each topic area before you move along, asking him "Is there anything that we've talked about so far that you'd like to know more about?" I tell my fieldwork attendees that we can have a brief conversation in front of the participant about any questions they have; they may want to suggest a topic to me rather than constructing the question directly themselves, which enables me to pick that question up or defer it as I choose. (For example, "Steve, I'd love to learn about how Jacob sends the documents to accounting.")

Much of this presumes that the fieldwork team is assembled from two types of people: those who are likely to be reading this book, and those who wouldn't even have imagined a book like this existed. Alternatively, if you are out in the field with a peer, and you've had a fair amount of experience, not only individually but also as a team, you will find a lovely fluidity between the two of you. Your brain will tell you, based on body language and breath, when your colleague wants to ask a question. If you are chasing down a bit of information, don't turn it over immediately; just make eye contact to let your partner know you're getting there, finish the thread you are exploring, and then give him the "nod" to step in. This can be a wonderful moment, where instead of feeling like you are managing precocious toddlers, you are instead gigging with a very tight jam band.

Be clear with yourself whether you are interviewing with a peer or managing a less-experienced fieldwork attendee. With a peer, your goal is to harness her keen brain and make the interview better. Talk to your peer before the interview and explore tactically how loose you both want to be. With a fieldwork attendee, you don't share a mental model about how the interview might proceed, and so he might be as baffled by your next question as you would be by his random question. Given that, your goal is to maintain control over the flow of the interview while facilitating the attendee to have a successful experience. Engaging him and uncovering his perspective (as revealed by his questions) is important as well, but I see that placing third.

Once You Get On-Site

Once you get on-site, you'll find these different stages:

1. Crossing the threshold

2. Restating objectives

3. Kick-off question

4. Accept the awkwardness

5. The tipping point

6. Reflection and projection

7. The soft close

In Chapter 3, "Getting Ready to Conduct Your Interviews," I described the general flow of most interview guides. The flow of the guide corresponds roughly to the stages of the interview.

Crossing the Threshold

The very first few moments of an on-site interview are often characterized by mild confusion, especially if you are going to someone's home; less so if you are arriving at a professional office with a reception area. In general, your participants aren't 100 percent clear on what's expected of them. They may not have been told, or remember, your name or the organization you represent, and only know the details of who recruited them to participate. Before you arrive, figure out what you are going to say. It may be as simple as "Hi, I'm Steve. I'm here for the interview." Or "Hi, I'm Steve from _____. I'm here for the interview." (These work especially well if your name happens to be Steve.) Think carefully about what organization name you use. They may know the recruiting firm's name (or even the name of the individual recruiter), but not the name of your company. They may be more familiar with your product's name (such as BlackBerry) than your organization's name (such as Research In Motion).[2] Identify yourself in a way that they'll recognize. Of course, if you've personally reached out to the participants by email or telephone before the interview, this is much simpler.

Whether you are in a home, a workplace, or any other environment, once you are "in," social graces matter. Introduce the rest of your fieldwork team and offer to take off your shoes if you are in someone's home (but be sure you don't have holes in your socks!). As you come in, figure out where you want to start the session. In an office, it may be a conference room. In a home, it may be the living room or dining table. Even if the bulk of the interview is going to take place at a specific location (say, at a computer or in the mail room), you may want to start off in a more open and front-stage part of the environment. Your participant won't know what you need, so be prepared to ask her.

Arrange seating so that you and your fellow interviewer (or interviewers) are near each other. In order to maximize the engagement among all parties, you want the fieldwork team to be able to maintain eye contact with the participant, and you want the participant to be able to respond to questions from either of you without having to turn her head too far (see Figure 5.2). If need be, ask the participant to sit in a particular spot. The participant doesn't know what's supposed to happen, so by gently taking charge, you can reassure her and set the tone for the whole interview.

If you're shooting video, make sure the lighting is appropriate. If your participant is sitting in front of a bright light (such as a window), then ask her to move or close a blind. If the room is too dark, ask about opening window coverings or turning on lights. If there's a radio or television on, ask her to turn it off (as sometimes those can appear more prominently on audio recordings than you would expect). This isn't a social visit (as a guest, you probably wouldn't ask your friend to move to a different seat), but rather it's

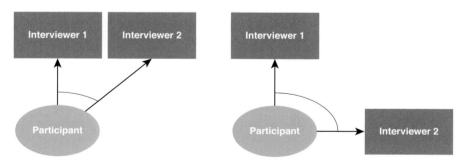

FIGURE 5.2
Ensure that all interviewers can maintain eye contact with the participant (L), rather than forcing her to swivel her head to keep you both in view (R).

2   In January 2013, Research in Motion finally acknowledged how people think of them and changed their organization's name to BlackBerry.

a purposeful, arranged session. If you are offered a drink, feel free to accept it, as this is the participant's way of anchoring the session to a familiar scenario. The participant isn't trained as a professional interviewee so she will, of course, rely on familiar styles of social interactions. Although it's fine for you to accept her social gestures (in some cases, it can be essential, as a failure to do so can be read as rude; err on the side of taking the offered glass of water), as the interviewer, you will offer fewer of those gestures yourself.

As you are settling into place and getting your gear unpacked and set up, ask the participant to sign any non-disclosure and consent agreements. I'll often bring it out as quickly as possible and tell the participant "Before we get started, we've just got some paperwork for you." The key words here are "Before we get started." Specifics will vary depending on the study, but in general, ethically and legally, the interview shouldn't start until your participant has signed whatever forms you've planned for. Let the forms do their work: don't project your own discomfort onto the participant by over-explaining the contents of the form. I prefer to hand over a pen and the forms and then sit quietly (or prepare my surroundings) while she reads it over. Defensive nattering ("Ha, ha, this won't end up on YouTube") undercuts the document's clarity and raises concerns that the participant might not even have. Start setting up the video camera or getting your field materials ready rather than watching her.

Sometimes the people who join me in the field will try to fill these initial moments with small talk that can inadvertently transition into some of the interview content itself. The participant—without a clear sense of the process—may start offering up opinions and details. Agree ahead of time with your colleagues not to let the small talk turn into questioning before you have the signed consent, and before you have your video camera (or other recording media) turned on. Otherwise, you're going to have to ask those questions again. Small talk is a lovely lubricant, but keep it at small talk—discuss the weather, or how your day is going, but don't start asking questions about artifacts in the environment or how long she has been doing her job.

Restating Objectives

This is the point at which the interview itself really begins. Thank the participant for taking the time to speak with you, and at a high level, tell her what this is about. This is an early and important chance for you to speak using her terminology, not yours. Depending on how her participation was secured, someone may have told her something about why you are doing this and what is being asked of her. If that someone wasn't you, you don't really know what was said. Even if it was you who spoke with the participant, you don't really know what she took away from the conversation.

It's okay to describe your work as "market research" if that's the most understandable way for her to know what you are doing. The differences between user research and design research and market research do not matter to her!

I refer to our process and objectives at a high level: "We're working for a technology company, and we're out talking to a bunch of different people about how they are using their laptops."

I sometimes acknowledge the recruiting process explicitly. Depending on the topic, it may have been very clear to the participant by the end of the screening interview what it was we were interested in, saying, "You probably know from the questions that we were asking when you talked with...that we're interested in..." or "I don't know how much you know about what we're doing. I know you answered a lot of questions about..."

Let the participant know what to expect by giving a thumbnail outline of the process: "We'll take about 90 minutes with you. We've got a bunch of questions to ask to start off, and then later it'd be great if you can show us the warehouse," or "Let's start here with some discussion and then we've got something we'd like to show you and get your feedback." If they have any concerns ("I have to stop at 2:15 to go pick up my daughter"), then these should come up right away, and you can adjust your process, timing, or clarify your expectations. This has the additional benefit of reminding your client (who maybe isn't as prepared as you'd like) what is going to happen.

Engage your participant: "Do you have any questions for us right now?" If she doesn't have questions, keep moving, because even though you've told her that you have specific questions for her, a participant may feel that it's up to her to somehow start telling what she thinks might address your objectives. You may even want to shut down too many detailed questions ("How many people are you meeting?" "What company do you work for?") by deferring those until the end of the interview. In a gentle way, you can use this to further set the tone for you as the leader of the interview.

> **NOTE** ADAPTING AT THE OUTSET
>
> Once, in interviews with high-powered fast-talking finance professionals, I found myself getting through about half of these first few sentences before they verbally brushed past me and launched into their complaints about our client's product (something we were all well aware of and not at all focused on for these interviews). Because of the difficulty of access to these customers (who were basically doing the interview as a favor), they didn't seem to have well-managed expectations about our goals. Eventually, I just turned this part of the interview over to them, kicking off by asking, "Well, before we start, why do *you* think we're here?" Inevitably, they politely raged about their current frustrations until I could interrupt with "Actually, we know that's important, but that's not what we're hoping to talk about today." It was not an orthodox way of starting the conversation, but given the type of people I was meeting and the context of their frustration, it was an effective adaptation.

by Julie Peggar

Julie Peggar is an ethnographer,
chief storyteller, and president,
Gaze Ethnographic Consulting, Inc.

I don't conduct interviews.

In my design-oriented working world, interviews form the basis of most research. For me,
this hasn't always been the case. I come from
a more traditional ethnographic background,

FIGURE 5.3
Julie Peggar

one in which interviewing is merely a by-product of being in a situation, rather
than the primary reason for the visit. When I design a study, I try to avoid formal,
stand-alone interviews as a part of the process. Instead, I ask what phenomenon
we're trying to understand, where I would have to be to see it in action, and who
the people might be who can get me there. I privilege observing and participating over asking and telling. A successful field visit is one in which, at the end,
the participant feels like they've made a new friend rather than like they've just
been interviewed.

When I first meet participants, they are often curious about what I do, who I am
as a person, and why I'm so interested in the mundane details of hanging out with
them while they do the dishes or pick up their kids. In the field, I don't put on a
"working personality." I'm just me, getting to know them and letting them get to
know me back. This give and take helps me blend into the environment more naturally, learning how they would introduce someone new into the family, business,
or activity. The process of getting to know one another gives me critical information about the culture and context within which my topic exists. I know I've done
my job building rapport when we've been talking for half an hour and someone
says, "I should shut up and stop asking you questions so you can start." We've

already started. Their interest in my world tells me about theirs. Everything is data to me, not just specific questions about specific objects or actions.

Although I have general areas of inquiry that I know I'd like to cover, I don't put limits on my time with the participant or on what we do in the time that I'm there. I've never spent less than an hour and a half on a visit, and my longest single visit (so far!) was 16 hours, although I've been based in field sites for months at a time. I allow what we cover to emerge from the day's activities, and my questions are firmly based in what I see them do or hear them say in context rather than on pre-existing ideas about what might arise. In practice, this works much better than it sounds! If a participant gets a phone call in the middle of a formal two-hour interview about GPS units, asking him to leave immediately and drive from San Francisco to Los Angeles that night, would he ask the interviewer to come with him? As an interviewer, would you go? What if instead of an interviewer, there was someone just hanging out and spending the day with you, who has as much time as it takes for you to teach them about your GPS unit? Would you ask then?

My research assistant and I were hanging out in San Francisco with a comic, learning how he uses his GPS to get to new venues. At some point during the evening, he got a call about a booking in Los Angeles for the next afternoon that he really wanted to do, even though he had to be back in San Francisco that same night. He asked if we wanted to come along...so we stayed with him. We drove down to Los Angeles with him that night in the pouring rain, in his beat-up car with no heater, and windshield wipers that didn't work, and his bright, shiny, new, expensive GPS on the dash! Then we went to his show the next afternoon and drove back home with him that evening. We certainly got a great idea of what his life is like, about his purchasing decisions and priorities, about the pros and cons involved in using the GPS on a long road trip that included both known and unknown roads, and about how the GPS fit into the overall picture. This was a lot of data that we would have missed out on with a more formal design.

Kick-Off Question

This is another transitional moment as you move into the body of the interview and begin to actively inhabit the role of the question-asker. Your intro words—"So, to start"—help move things forward, past small talk and logistics. The first question is usually a simple broad one to set some context.

"Maybe introduce yourself and tell us about what your job is here?" It doesn't matter too much what it is, as you are going to follow up with many more specific questions. The key here is not to start too specifically ("Ahem. Question 1. What are the top features you desire in your mobile device?"), but to be mindful of shifting into the mode of asking questions.

Accept the Awkwardness

As you proceed through your questions, you may encounter some resistance. Although many people (especially those likely to agree to participate) will be extroverted and comfortable, some people will be uncomfortable. There's no formula for how long it takes people to get past discomfort. Some people will get there with you in a few minutes, whereas others may take an hour. Sometimes (rarely, in my experience), they'll never reach that point. This discomfort presents itself in subtle ways; rather than frowns and squirming, you may observe stiff posture and clipped deliberate responses. They may fend off your questions (while seemingly answering them) by implying that those are not normal things to be asking about, or providing little or no detail about themselves, describing their behavior as "you know, just regular."

You may have to identify your own feelings of discomfort to know when you're in this stage. If you feel like you don't have permission to keep going, or that this person doesn't really want you there, you are in this stage. First, you have to accept this as awkward. It's not the worst thing in the world to be conversing with someone and feeling ill at ease. You aren't in physical peril; it's just an inner feeling. Let it happen, but don't let it define you. Listen to the feeling and set it aside. Now give your participant plenty of ways to succeed. Ask her easy questions, keeping the inquiry factual, straightforward, and simple. This isn't the time to ask challenging questions or to bring out props or stimuli. Be patient and keep asking questions and keep accepting, acknowledging, and appreciating her responses. Your own comfort (or discomfort) will come through and contribute to the tone. If you're following your field guide linearly, you may get a good portion of the way through in a short time and begin to feel some panic about the amount of questions you've come with. Just stick with it; the remaining questions will take longer to get through (and will generate more follow-up questions, too).

The Tipping Point

Although I can't predict when it will happen, there's often a point when the participant shifts from giving short answers to telling stories (see Figure 5.4). Whether or not it's an actual moment where the answers get longer, there is a point where you realize that you've arrived at a high level of rapport and the tenor of the exchange is different. In all likelihood, by the time you have that realization, you've probably been crossing back and forth between short answers and stories. Even if you do notice more short answers, you are on your way, so just stick with what you've been doing.

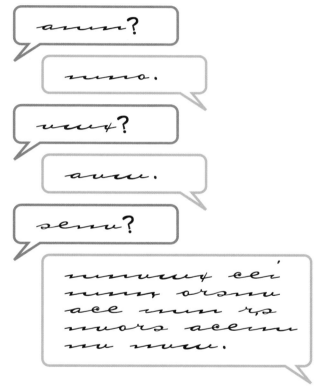

FIGURE 5.4
You can see where this hypothetical interview tips from questions and answers into stories.

Reflection and Projection

The deepest rapport comes when the participant has spent enough time immersed in the topic in a supportive and exploratory fashion. By this time, you've presumably captured many of the details around process, behaviors, usage, and so on, and are ready to move into the higher-level part of the inquiry. Now your participant is thinking about the big picture. Her responses drift into sweeping statements about herself, her goals, her dreams, her past, the future, our society, and so on. This is the type of thing that varies across cultures. Anecdotally, I suspect this may be a more American characteristic than, say, British. This can be the most fun part of the interview; it's certainly the most inspiring. You are now fully drawn into her world, and she is painting a detailed picture of what lies beneath or what lies beyond.

Just because people are speaking about a future (say, how mobile phones will change their relationships) doesn't mean it's an accurate prediction. That's not the point of the question; it's what these predictions and reflections reveal. These parts of the interview often produce phrases or ideas that the field team will continue to repeat and go back to as they distill complex issues into visionary notions.

The Soft Close

Assuming that your participant isn't running off to another appointment, the winding-down of the interview can be a soft process. Your hard cues (thanking her, handing her the incentive, packing up your stuff, standing up) may not mean she is going to stop talking. Physicians and therapists are familiar with the "doorknob phenomenon," where crucial information is revealed just as the patient is about to depart. So consider keeping your recording device on, even if it's packed up. Even as you are heading to the door, the interview may resume, at the participant's initiation. Or you may see something in the environment to ask about. Keep your eyes and brain in interview mode until you are fully departed. Even if you are tired and ready to leave, stifle the inner "Oh, there's nothing here" voice that wants you to pull the plug. Stick with it a couple of minutes more. Those may be the bits of recorded data that pull the whole project together for you in the analysis phase. You don't know at this point!

Summary

Although interviews are all wonderfully unique, they tend to follow a consistent pattern. Each stage requires specific tactical preparation or responses from you, the interviewer. With experience, moving through the different stages will become second nature.

- When you first come in, set up your seating so the participant can easily maintain eye contact with *all* interviewers. Use just enough small talk but don't get bogged down in chat. If you are offered a drink, feel free to accept it.

- If you are joined by colleagues or clients who aren't skilled at interviewing, manage their participation by giving them tasks (for example, photographing the interview) or by briefing them on when to ask questions and what kind of questions they should be asking.

- Start with a general, easy question (such as asking the participant to introduce herself). Ideally, the rest of the interview just flows from there as follow-up questions.

- If your participant exhibits discomfort, you can choose whether or not you feel discomfort yourself in response. If you feel uncomfortable, you should find a way to accept that feeling as just a feeling and move forward.

- People will respond with short answers at first and will eventually reach a point where they are telling stories. You can't predict how long it will take to reach that point, but that *is* the goal.

- Remember the "doorknob phenomenon," where people suddenly open up as the session ends. Try to keep recording until you're out the door.

CHAPTER 6

How to Ask Questions

So there you are in "the field," that coolest of phrases that means that today your assignment is to talk with a stranger in her kitchen, maintenance shed, copy center, or other unlikely environment. As you get down to business, your printed copy of the field guide is gripped tightly in your sweaty paw. All your objective-setting, question-wordsmithing, and other planning is captured in 11-point type on these precious four sheets of paper.

Now, set it aside.

Leading the interview successfully comes down to *you*. Go ahead and refer to the field guide as you need to, but don't let it run the interview. It's not a script; it's only for reference purposes. If you get stuck about where to go next, that's when you pull it out and scan through the pages. Despite your planning, the interview probably won't unfold the way you anticipated. If it does, perhaps you aren't leveraging the opportunities that arise. If you're a novice interviewer, you'll probably lean more toward the guide than improvisation. Similarly, if you're at the very beginning of a study, you should rely more on the guide than you will once you've learned from a couple of interviews.

> **TIP** HOLD ONTO YOUR LOOSE-LEAF
>
> Keep your field guide in a portfolio, a folder, a sheaf of papers, a notebook, or something else. You'll be better off if the guide appears to be put away when you aren't using it. Early on I did an interview with the field guide held out in front of me as my only bit of "business." At one point, my participant snatched it from my hands and said, "Okay, what else do you wanna know?" Although this is unlikely to happen often, it served as a good lesson for me to tote my paraphernalia in a more professional (and protected) manner.

Silence Defeats Awkwardness

After you ask a question, be silent. This is tricky; you are speaking with someone you've never spoken to before. You are learning about her conversational rhythm, how receptive she is to your questions, and what cues she gives when thinking about an answer. These tiny moments—from part of a second to several seconds—are nerve-wracking. One way a novice interviewer tries to counteract nervousness is by preemptively filling the silence. So the interviewer asks long questions. What he wants to know is, "What did you have for breakfast yesterday?" but the novice stretches the question out so as to delay that moment where the question is done, and he is forced to await the answer (or some awful unnamed fate). The question then becomes "What did you have for breakfast yesterday...was it toast or juice?" The novice interviewer is suggesting possible responses, and his interviewee is just that much more likely to work within the interviewer's suggestions rather than offer up her own answers. In fact, what the novice interviewer probably asked was, "What did you have for breakfast yesterday? Was it toast, or juice, or…?" You can hear the novice interviewer actually articulate the ellipsis, as a descending, slowly fading "Rrrrrrr?" That trailing sound is the last gasp at holding onto the question

Don't do this. Ask your question and let it stand. Be deliberate about this. To deal with your (potentially agonizing!) discomfort during the silence, give yourself something to do—slowly repeat "allow silence" as many times as it takes. Use this as a mantra to calm and clear your mind (at least for the moment). If the person can't answer the question, she will let you know.

After she has given you an answer, continue to be silent. People speak in paragraphs, and they want your permission to go on to the next paragraph. You ask "What did you have for breakfast yesterday?" There's a second of silence, and the person tells you, "I had toast and a bit of yogurt, and then about 20 minutes later, I had steak and eggs." Our novice interviewer figures it's time to move on to the next question, asking "Oh, okay. Where did you buy those groceries?" But the best play is to just rest for another beat. Usually, the person will continue. "Well, in fact, yesterday was quite unusual because what I typically do is just have a granola bar, but my sister was coming to visit, and I had to prepare for all of us before she got here." By simply not asking your next question, you can give your interviewee time to flesh out the answer they've already given you. Try to sense when the thread is played out, and it's time for your next question.

> **TIP** PARAGRAPH SPEAK
>
> People do speak in paragraphs. You can see evidence of this by looking at an interview transcription. The pauses between blocks of content are interpreted by the transcriptionist as paragraphs.

Werner Herzog's documentary *Grizzly Man* tells the story of Timothy Treadwell, a self-professed naturalist who lived in the wilderness to be close to his beloved grizzly bears, only to be mauled to death. There's a scene in which Franc Fallico, Alaska's state medical examiner, presents a watch, still in an evidence bag, to Treadwell's ex-girlfriend, Jewel Palovak. Herzog, holding the camera, cuts between passively observing the dialogue between the two of them and inserting his own questions about her memory of Treadwell (and his girlfriend who died with him). Finally, Fallico has Jewel sign some official papers, and the process is complete. Herzog doesn't cut and continues to film the two. But nothing is happening! They have uttered their concluding words and smile awkwardly and stare at nothing. Moments tick by and still no cutting. Jewel gives a sharp intake of breath, and Herzog, holding the camera, steps forward. Another moment goes by, and she sobs, breaking down for the first time in this entire sequence. "It's the last thing that's left." Herzog is directing the scene while observing and interviewing. He lets a delicate moment hang uncomfortably, and a devastating emotion emerges. That's the power of silence.

Even if you don't feel nervous, you can't really know what's going to happen as you ask a question.[1] Perhaps your participant will start to answer the question while you are asking it (indeed, you can see this sometimes when the participant's whole affect changes as he begins to understand the question and his face shifts dramatically as he brings his answer out to the launch pad). Perhaps he'll be supremely fast-talking[2] and whip out an answer the very moment you've finished asking it. Perhaps he will wait for you to finish your question and take some amount of time to start speaking, and during that gulf between question and answer he may give you really great "I'm thinking" cues (hand rubs chin, eyes gaze away, lips pursed, and so on). Perhaps he'll give you a juicy verbal cue, like "That's a great question...ummmm...." Or he may simply stare at you, giving no quarter, until he answers. Be prepared for any of these!

With some participants, it takes me most of the interview to align my pacing with theirs. I'm particularly vulnerable to what one might call the Skype effect. When technology (VOIP, Skype, transatlantic cables, satellite transmission, and so on) introduces a small delay in conversation, we get messed up pretty quickly; the pauses we listen for at the end of someone's speech are not quite in real time and so we start to speak at the same time as the person on the other end of the call. We hear each other start and so we abruptly stop and defer to them. It's challenging to correct this out-of-phase state. Of course, this happens in person as well, without any technologically introduced delay. Some people just have different natural rhythms. There's no magic fix, any more than there's an easy way to successfully talk on the phone when you hear an echo of your own voice. This is stuff happening way below conscious thought, down at the autonomic level. At the very least, be mindful of the out-of-sync phenomenon and try to slow...yourself...down.

Managing the Flow

At a high level, most of the interview can unfold naturally from the kickoff question (see Chapter 5, "Key Stages of the Interview"). Strive to weave the questions from your field guide into follow-up questions. Although it won't cover the entirety of the interview, pursuing this ideal will help develop

---

1 Detailed analysis of "turn taking" is part of conversation analysis, a subdiscipline of linguistics. Experts explore how intonation, pausing, and body language inform the interaction between speakers. Unlike your work as an interviewer, conversation analysts don't do their work in real time.

2 A wonderful example is the rapid-fire dialogue between Hildy and Burns in the 1940 Howard Hawks film *His Girl Friday*.

rapport, demonstrate listening, and create an interaction that feels more conversational than interrogatory.

Not everything can be a follow-up. Some threads run out of steam, or sometimes you need to deliberately change the discussion in order to dig into a specific area of interest. The guiding principle here is to *signal your lane changes*. Compare these two snippets of a hypothetical interview:

Version 1

> **Q:** And what happened when you downloaded the updated version of the iPhone app?
>
> **A:** (laughs) It installed instantly!
>
> **Q:** Where do you keep your used oil drums?

Version 2

> **Q:** And what happened when you downloaded the updated version of the iPhone app?
>
> **A:** (laughs) It installed instantly!
>
> **Q:** Okay, this is great. I'm just going to shift direction here. Maybe you can tell us, where do you keep your used oil drums?

In the second snippet, the deliberate, explicit turn signal acknowledges the most recent answer and points the way toward the next, otherwise discontinuous, topic for discussion. As a rule, if your question isn't fairly obviously a follow-up question, you should preface it with some transitional words.

Getting to Even More of the Answer

Here's some bad news: you won't get the answer to your questions just by asking. If only you could simply utter the question and wait while the person gives you all the information you need, and then move on to the next question on your list. That's just not how real interviews go. For most threads in most interviews, you need to use a series of questions to get to the information you want. It's not that people are being difficult; they just don't know what it is that you want to know. They interpret your question in a certain way and do their best to answer it. But it's up to you to help them to tell you what you need to learn about.

When you listen to your participant answering your question, be vigilant. Do they appear to have understood what you intended by the question, or have they gone somewhere else with it? Their interpretation may be more revealing than what you intended, so you may just let the conversation go down that path, or you might want to wait for an appropriate time to redirect back to the topic you were initially interested in.

by Lynn Shade

Lynn Shade is a freelance UX designer and researcher who previously worked at Claris, Apple, and Adobe. She grew up in Japan and is bilingual.

Over the course of my career, most of the user research I've done has been in Asia, in large part in Japan, where I happened to grow up and where software companies used to invest in efforts to understand market needs. Years ago when working for Apple, I accompanied a Dutch colleague, Anke de Jong, to New York for field research for new laptop models. Trained as an industrial designer, Anke designed at the intersection of hardware and software. This made her research interesting in and of itself, but what I remember most vividly from that trip was being occasionally astonished at her use of silence to impel further comment.

FIGURE 6.1

Lynn Shade

This technique wasn't for the most part necessary since as compared to Asian participants, these participants talked a lot. Admittedly, we were interviewing New Yorkers, but the willingness and eagerness of American study participants to express themselves verbally was the source of considerable discussion and hidden envy among myself and my Japanese colleagues. In Silicon Valley at the time, the solo-participant-in-a-lab Talk Aloud methodology was enjoying great popularity as the de-facto usability testing methodology. Upper management expected this quick lab technique would be used to inexpensively confirm U.S. results in other countries. Doing research in Japan wasn't so easy. Beleaguered by the all-too-common silent-ish Japanese participant, Japanese colleagues and I would discuss endlessly and even devote entire conference presentations to how to draw our quiet participants out, and what magic combination of factors might encourage them to speak.

However, even Americans can go silent after answering a question. If this happened, Anke would deliberately not comment, waiting calmly and putting what seemed to me subtle stress on the interviewee. The first few times I observed this, the Japanese part of me would grow slightly anxious as the silence hung in the air for a half-beat too long. Invariably, the interviewee would break it. The additional information was often valuable; they'd clarify or amend, or start a new topic with a new observation, or make a connection that offered interesting insights. The interviewees, while feeling the need to break the silence, seemed not to mind. They often became very talkative, responding to the silence as the encouragement it was.

Using silence as a mechanism to elicit participants to talk is a common technique, but it stuck in my head. Over the years as I continued doing research in Asia, I thought quite a bit about that New York experience and silence in general. Silence in user research in Japan is so important. We allowed lots and lots of room for it. There have been entire books written on Japanese silence, but for the purposes of this sidebar I'll summarize Japanese conversational silence into three broad categories: setting-the-stage silence, effort silence, and failure silence.

- **Setting-the-stage silence:** Along with body language, setting-the-stage silence is a spot of silence from both sides to indicate readiness for a shared experience. Both parties work to set the mood for a productive conversation, and some of this work is done with silence. This silence takes place here and there during initial greetings, along the way as topics change, and is most obvious when greetings wind down right before initiating the topic at hand. Lest this paint the wrong picture of some prolonged zazen meditation-like situation with a temple bell tolling in the background, let me hasten to add that those setting-the-stage silences can be long or quick, depending on personalities. Fairly typical in lots of situations is saying the equivalent of "um" with a trailing silence and the other party nodding, again followed by a bit of silence. Setting-the-stage silence is created partly because silence is considered a more deeply shared experience than talking—a version of that exists in many cultures—and partly showing mutual respect and mutual humility for the other's expertise. The interviewer's task here and during the interview is to match the interviewee's natural response and thought pace, allowing time for both sides to ponder questions.

- **Effort silence:** During the interview, silence indicates making an effort to help the cause along. The interviewee will be silent to show they're thinking the topic over carefully and showing a desire to contribute to the interviewer's goal. The interviewer will be silent to show they're thinking the subject's response over carefully and showing respect for the effort the interviewee made in answering. All parties may be silent when faced with a very difficult or complex question to show respect for the difficulty by giving it due diligence and giving the question and the other parties room to think. Essentially, Japanese people are being conversationally encouraging by using lots of silence.

- **Failure silence:** The tones of silence to watch for are silence indicating resistance and silence indicating confusion. If the interviewees don't feel knowledgeable enough or qualified to answer the question, they'll fall silent. Likewise, when confused by a question and unsure, interviewees can fall silent. This "falling silent" has its own tiny cues and must be broken by interjections from the interviewer. If the failure silence is overly prolonged, the interviewee will start experiencing the stress of failure. This is why the waiting-without-help technique used so successfully in New York wouldn't work in Japan, at least not without considerable modification.

The designer Kenya Hara has a rather lovely section in his book *White* on the meaning of emptiness in the Shinto shrine architecture. He describes how the space created by tying the tops of four pillars with ropes creates emptiness that has potential as a vessel to receive thoughts and feelings. He later goes on to tie silence to emptiness and suggests that silence has the possibility to enrich mutual comprehension. Building on this, it's hard to imagine silence in Japanese conversation as being created simply to facilitate a means to a certain end. Rather, successful Japanese silence is a roomy empty space that, created by both parties, helpfully exists to allow communication.

Is there more that you need to probe further on? People sometimes speak in coded terms: "...this was before the earlier situation that changed my purchasing...." The "earlier situation" may be something they are uncomfortable revealing, at least for now, or it may be that they aren't sure if they have your permission to share the specifics of the "earlier situation." Even if you don't follow up immediately, it may be a topic you want to return to.

Are you asking the question in a way they can answer? In a study about customer service, a participant complained passionately about the poor telephone service he received from a retailer. I asked him how the service might be different, but he could only speak about the current situation. Eventually I shifted my tactics entirely, and we role-played an imagined future version of the telephone interactions. My follow-up questions focused on uncovering the specific details that made his scenario a desirable one.

A Palette of Question Types

The field guide is your (highly idealized) hypothesis for how you will ask questions. But really, you'll spend much of your effort in the interview digging further and giving your participant the best opportunity to share deeply. You need a broad set of question types in order to make this happen. Here are some examples to get you started:

Questions that gather context and collect details:

- **Ask about sequence.** "Describe a typical workday. What do you do when you first sit down at your station? What do you do next?"

- **Ask about quantity.** "How many files would you delete when that happens?"

- **Ask for specific examples.** "What was the last movie you streamed?" Compare that question to "What movies do you stream?" The specific is easier to answer than the general and becomes a platform for follow-up questions.

- **Ask about exceptions.** "Can you tell me about a time when a customer had a problem with an order?"

- **Ask for the complete list.** "What are all the different apps you have installed on your smartphone?" This will require a series of follow-up questions—for example, "What else?" Very few people can generate an entire list of something without some prompting.

- **Ask about relationships.** "How do you work with new vendors?" This general question is especially appropriate when you don't even know enough to ask a specific question (such as in comparison to the earlier example about streaming movies). Better to start general than to be presumptive with a too-specific question.

- **Ask about organizational structure.** "Who do the people in that department report to?"

Questions that probe what's been unsaid:

- **Ask for clarification.** "When you refer to 'that,' you are talking about the newest server, right?"

- **Ask about code words/native language.** "Why do you call it the *bat cave*?"

- **Ask about emotional cues.** "Why do you laugh when you mention Best Buy?"

- **Ask why.** "I've tried to get my boss to adopt this format, but she just won't do it...." "Why do you think she hasn't?"

- **Probe delicately.** "You mentioned a difficult situation that changed your usage. Can you tell me what that situation was?"

- **Probe without presuming.** "Some people have very negative feelings about the current government, while others don't. What is *your* take?" Rather than the direct "What do you think about our government?" or "Do you like what the government is doing lately?" This indirect approach offers options associated with the generic "some people" rather than the interviewer or the interviewee.

- **Explain to an outsider.** "Let's say that I've just arrived here from another decade, how would you explain to me the difference between smartphones and tablets?"

- **Teach another.** "If you had to ask your daughter to operate your system, how would you explain it to her?"

Questions that create contrasts in order to uncover frameworks and mental models:

- **Compare processes.** "What's the difference between sending your response by fax, mail, or email?"

- **Compare to others.** "Do the other coaches also do it that way?"

- **Compare across time.** "How have your family photo activities changed in the past five years? How do you think they will be different five years from now?" The second question is not intended to capture an accurate prediction. Rather, the question serves to break free from what exists now and envision possibilities that may emerge down the road. Identify an appropriately large time horizon (A year? Five years? Ten years?) that helps people to think beyond incremental change.

A while back I was in my first public improv show. We were all amateurs, some with many years of experience, others with a year or less (such as me). In this performance, we started each scene with one idea (often from the audience) and proceeded with some sort of structure. What often happened was a scramble to move the idea forward—everyone speaking at once, with too many ideas "thrown" in the first few moments to ever really solidify into a great scene. Have you ever seen 8-year-olds play soccer? The ball and both teams are a whirling cloud that moves up and down and across the field like the Tasmanian Devil. That was us.

But then the next night I saw the Kids in the Hall—a comedy troupe that has been performing together for a very long time. After the scripted material had finished, the audience was clamoring for more. In advance of the encore, they all walked on stage and thanked us, and then improvised a few jokes before heading off stage to prepare for the encore. All five of them managed to hold the stage coherently. Not everyone spoke at equal length in those few minutes, but at no point did any of them speak on top of another. It came off as natural and easy, but it was really quite incredible.

Where they succeeded, and we didn't succeed as well (for there are no losers in improv) was in allowing for silence. Each Kid in the Hall was silent for most, if not all, of their unscripted segment. What a powerful contribution they made by not speaking. Isn't that a strange statement to make? A comedy performer contributed by not speaking. How can that be? We tend to expect performance to be the explicit utterances, not the space between them.

There's a lot that can happen without verbalization—posture, gestures, breath sounds, eye gaze, facial reactions, and more. The Kids in the Hall were doing all those the entire time—and they were paying attention to each other. When they were silent, they were actively silent; they were sending and receiving information.

This behavior is crucial when interviewing users. I would estimate we speak as little as 20 percent of the time. Yet the interviews are directed and controlled by the interviewer. Nodding, eye contact, and body language all support the respondent in providing detailed information.

Of course, there is often more than one researcher on hand. If the first ethnographer remains silent, waiting for the respondent to continue, the second interviewer must recognize that, and also listen silently, rather than using the opening as his chance to interview. This collaborative use of silence is something the Kids in the Hall managed, and my improv group did not.

We experience these same challenges in more familiar work settings: brainstorming, meetings, and so on. We work in a society that judges us primarily by our own contributions, rather than the way we allow others to make theirs. If the collaborative silence is not a shared value in a group, there can be a real challenge for those who default to listening, not speaking. We've learned how to give credit to those who utter the pearls, but we don't know how to acknowledge the value of those who choose their moments wisely, who allow others to shine, and who ultimately enable those pearls.

In a 2002 episode of The Simpsons (DABF05, "Jaws Wired Shut"), Homer's jaw is wired shut. He is physically unable to speak. He does become a better listener, but most interesting are the positive qualities the people in his life project upon him. Simpsons' Executive Producer Al Jean said: "When Homer gets his jaw wired shut, it makes him into a really decent, wonderful human being." I don't know if Al Jean is getting post-modern on us, but Homer's internal change, through his silence, was fairly minor compared to the differences that other people perceived. For even more on this theme, check out the book *Being There* by Jerzy Kozinsky (or the film with Peter Sellers).

Managing the Ebb and Flow of the Interview

As a plan for an idealized interview, the field guide is, of course, linear. But the active planning process you go through during the interview is actually more of a tree (see Figure 6.2).

This is a fairly typical snippet of an interview. It's what is going on for the interviewer that deserves some special focus here, though. As the participant is explaining in his natural manner, the interviewer is identifying other questions to ask. At the first pause, the interviewer has at least two new questions (beyond what's already in her interview guide), but the questions encourage the participant to continue by responding with "Okay." As the participant continues, she might identify another two topics to be explored. Maybe those topics are included in the interview guide, but probably they aren't.

Sadly, most of us are constrained by the linearity of time. We can't clone ourselves and follow each thread in parallel universes. We have to stick with our own reality.

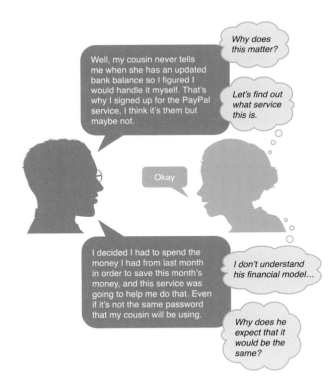

FIGURE 6.2
Even in this tiny excerpt of an interview, the interviewer has to track a great deal of information and make choices about where to go next.

In addition to watching the clock, maintaining eye contact, building rapport, and so on for most of the interview, your job also includes managing this tree. Here are some coping techniques:

1. Wait patiently until these threads come up again in conversation organically, without you having to ask. Often they do.

2. Jot quick notes on your field guide about what you want to come back to, so you don't forget.

3. Prioritize (or perhaps *triage*) based on your research objectives. Although something that seems irrelevant does often prove to be insightful, you have to choose. So be opportunistic and choose what you think is going to bear fruit for your area of inquiry.

4. Triage based on what makes the best follow-up, in order to demonstrate listening and further the rapport.

   Come back to a topic later if it still seems important; refer back to the participant's previous statement in order to establish continuity. ("Earlier you mentioned using PayPal. I wanted to ask a bit more about that.")

TIP GOING WITH THE FLOW

The complexity embedded within the exploding questions tree might suggest that interviewing really sucks. In fact, dealing with these challenges can take you to someplace very creative. Mihály Csíkszentmihályi has articulated the psychological notion of *flow*— as "the mental state of operation in which a person in an activity is fully immersed in a feeling of energized focus, full involvement, and success in the process of the activity."[3] This certainly happens to me in interviews. My brain is firing on all cylinders with all the responsibilities I'm managing, and yet I can feel myself slow right down. It's a feeling in both my brain and my body, which compares to the familiar special effect, often seen through the view screen when a spaceship enters hyperspace and the stars stretch out from points into lines. In this calmness, I'm not ignoring the complexity; instead, I'm somehow above it. Things become very quiet in my head, and I can feel myself riding on top of the challenges of the interview. It's not boredom; it's a very engaged feeling. It's the opposite of the chicken-sans-head feeling you might imagine the demands of an interview could lead to. This flow state both creates and is fed by the imperative to keep silent, keep myself out of the equation, and let the experience breathe, while still being the most creative and insightful time during fieldwork.

---

3 http://en.wikipedia.org/wiki/Flow_(psychology)

Embracing Your Participant's Worldview

In Chapter 2, I introduced the principle of embracing how participants see their world. That principle informs the entire approach of a study, but it becomes vital once you are with that participant and asking questions. In this section, you'll see how to ensure that your questions make it clear to both you and your participant that you are curious, even hungry, to understand their worldview.

Use Their Language

Years ago I was working with a client on understanding the opportunities for a new home entertainment technology, targeting everyday consumers. We were in the family's home to speak with them about their current gear and how they were using it.

In this house, the father had put a lot of effort into making product choices that would enhance their family's time together. He was visibly (and appropriately) proud of their setup. As he explained the choices he had made, he explained how he didn't want a DVR, because of his concerns over privacy. He referred to the leading DVR brand, TiVo, but mispronounced it as "Tye-vo."

"I took a look at Tye-vo, but didn't want anyone paying attention to what we watch the way Tye-vo does so I decided that Tye-vo wasn't for us." As with many stories, this one has become richer in the retelling, but you can imagine how my client, originally an engineer, quietly winced each time the brand name was misspoken. I could sense his winces without turning my head to look at him.

The interview continued and when it was appropriate for me to ask follow-up questions about DVRs, I referred to it as the participant did—as Tye-vo. But later, when the client asked some of his own questions, he pronounced TiVo correctly as "tee-vo." This was a small, yet dramatic moment in the interview. This proud man was revealed to be, well, stupid, in front of his family, in his home. Despite being a self-proclaimed expert in these types of products, he was indirectly corrected and thus lowered in status. You could immediately feel the power dynamic in the room shift; now we were the experts, and he was just some dude. Of course, that's not the situation I was hoping for!

My client was a wonderful, sweet, caring person who would never dream of making this participant feel that badly. But it would have never occurred to him to say something the "wrong" way. Yet in this situation, it was right to be wrong. It wasn't our role to be right.

Design researcher Todd Hausman talks about his work on an instant messaging product, when research participants would refer to "emochicons." In reflecting back their pronunciation, he was viscerally reminded of the risk in making assumptions about users.

Letting go of being right is something to pay attention to in most interviews; it doesn't have to be as glaring a situation as a participant's mispronunciation of a technology or a brand name. It could be in the description of a part, a process, or just about anything. Even if there's not an obvious "right" or "wrong" way to refer to something, you must defer to the participant's way.

TIP WHEN IT'S AWKWARD TO USE THEIR LANGUAGE

It can be challenging to use someone else's terminology and feel as if you are being authentic. (After all, you are trying to establish rapport, and being fake would destroy that.) Participants in a study told us about a new technology that was being developed at their organization, called an *aggregator*. Due to its troubled history, it was referred to colloquially as an "aggravator." This term was used more frequently in the interview than "aggregator." But it wasn't comfortable for our interviewer to ask about the "aggravator." They didn't really have permission from the group to use their insider language, and they ran the risk of coming off as flippant or minimizing the seriousness of the development effort. They resolved it by acknowledging the participant's language and their own reluctance to use the same phrase. Going a little meta (such as "I want to ask about what you like to call the aggravator") enables the interviewer to point to the language directly, acknowledging the participant's terminology, as well as referring back to the previous conversation about the terminology itself. When the words being used become a topic in the interview, pointing to the words in this manner is appropriate.

In one project, a research participant referred to a technology platform their firm uses. Our client, perhaps trying to demonstrate insider status and reassure the participant that this interview was valid, asked about the platform but used an abbreviated form (in essence, a nickname) of the platform name. The participant responded by hesitantly using this nickname and then immediately correcting himself and switching back to the full name that he had originally used. If my client simply *had* to introduce his alternative name for the technology, he could have asked "Oh, when you say [platform name], I wonder if that's the same thing I'm used to calling [nickname]?" In this case, there would be no ambiguity, and he would not in any way be trying to clarify, so the better course of action would have been to build rapport by accepting the terms the participant was using rather than trying to demonstrate credibility.

Assume Your Participant Makes Sense

You may hear and see apparent contradictions. People may tell you they value cleanliness and then open a bedroom door to reveal piles of dirty clothes on the floor. Or people may express a preference for a certain type of feature and then reject an example you show them. Although you might find this frustrating, try to see it as an opportunity. Your interpretation of "cleanliness" may be oversimplified. The social performance of valuing cleanliness may be entirely separate than the act of maintaining cleanliness. Your framework for what that feature is doing may not align with the participant's framework. These seeming disconnects are indications that you need to explore further. This isn't about calling out hypocrisy; it's about probing to understand.

Don't Make Your Questions Pass/Fail

A client joined me in the field, arriving at our pre-meeting with mere moments to get acquainted and review the approach. This was not an ideal arrangement (and a good learning moment for me) and led to a dysfunctional dynamic. Her abrupt questions for our participant were presented more as tests than as inquiries. She asked our participant if she knew what a USB cable was (see Figure 6.3), phrasing it as a challenge rather than as something she was curious about. Later, she presented her framework for the digital media functionality she was charged with designing and asked the participants if they understood the difference between the various terms used in the framework. As an exercise, imagine asking someone if they know what a USB is. You might even try this out loud. First, ask in a gentle, curious fashion. Next, ask in a judgmental critical tone. In this case, my client was somewhere in between, but far too close to the critical side of the continuum for comfort. The participant became confused and very uncertain about how to talk about her usage since these terms were indeed unfamiliar. It's good to understand if the language you are using internally aligns with the way people are really talking, but that doesn't mean you need to thrust your terms at people and test them on whether or not they can explain them.

FIGURE 6.3
Do *you* know what a USB cable is?

Don't Presume They Accept Your Worldview

I interviewed a young man who had gone through a significant personal change, first living abroad as a successful professional, and then returning to California to live in his parents' home to go back to school. At one point in the interview, my client commented to our participant (let's call him Keith) about the differences in value systems between "Old Keith" and "New Keith." Even though this is not a framework that Keith had explicitly articulated to us, he said, "Right."

After a few minutes of further dialogue, I decided it was time to intercede, and I asked Keith what he thought about this idea of the old versus new Keith. Given the chance to expound, Keith told us, "I don't really see it."

At no point had Keith told us that he had old and new versions of himself. Keith was always Keith. My client was synthesizing on-the-fly and had imposed his model on Keith. And what did Keith do? He agreed. Of course he agreed! Why should he argue about something like that? Just because a framework isn't rejected by the participant doesn't mean it is accurate!

In an episode of Marc Maron's WTF podcast,[4] he spoke with 85-year-old comedy legend Jonathan Winters. Within this interview are several examples that embody the points I've made throughout this chapter—getting to more of the answer, asking clarification questions, managing the ebb and flow of the interview, and not presuming that the participant accepts the interviewer's worldview.

Early in the interview, Maron asked a fairly direct question:

You were in the Marines. Where were you?

Winters answered:

I went in at 17. The Japanese were way down on the list...Pearl Harbor. I didn't get along with either parent; they were divorced; it didn't seem to matter; they didn't like me.

His truth-in-comedy comment about his parents seemed to be a non-sequitur, and he continued on about his parents and some of his time in the Marines for more than three minutes (finally explaining that he was on an aircraft carrier, which answered Maron's question), before concluding with:

But I enjoyed the Marines...I only made corporal, but that's okay...

Maron picked up on the earlier non-sequitur and asked:

Was it a way to get out of your parents house?

And Winters quipped back:

Yeah, yeah, they were eager to sign. I never saw two people sign papers so fast!

---

4   Hear the whole episode at http://rfld.me/QLhHj5.

Although the answer to Maron's question was buried within several layers of stories, Winters only *implied* his motivation for enlisting. Maron did the right thing and asked his subject explicitly about it. As the interviewer, you want to find out for sure, from the subject's perspective, rather than leaving things to your own inferences.

Later in the interview, Maron was less successful as an interviewer. Winters described an early job working as a radio DJ. In this job, he eventually got bored and did interviews with himself, playing different characters. Management objected, Winters persisted, and he was fired:

Winters: *I did try some more guests and that was the end of that career there.*

Maron (laughing, interjected): *You had to, though, right?*

Winters: *I had to.*

Maron: *Yeah! It felt too good, right?*

Winters: *It felt good. I did a year there, and then I went to Columbus.*

Maron's interjections reflected his own interpretation: that Winters must have been compelled to continue doing interviews with himself because of how good it felt. Winters never actually said that, but Maron stated it as a fact, where his "right?" was not truly a question but more like a fellow bar patron elbowing you in the ribs while asking you to agree with him. What this transcription failed to capture was the momentum Winters had in telling his story, and even though he agreed with Maron, he was sidetracked from his story and ended up expressing parts of it in Maron's terms, not his own.

Don't Enter Lecture Mode

An alternative title here might be "Sit on your hands!" or "You don't need to give voice to every thought that comes into your head!" On a project that dealt with online decision support tools, one client, when offered the chance partway through the interview to follow up on the conversation so far, came up with this gem, presented here in sanitized form.

> I suppose that seems more like a divergent set of factors informing you versus specific feedback that came from any particular individual source and that served as a guiding factor for decisions for your purchase or not. I'm just thinking that it's more of a multiple...

At this point, the participant interrupted the client to tell us more about her decision-making process. Although sharing your forming thoughts *can* be a method of interrogation, it is a tricky approach, relying heavily on rapport and shared agenda to be effective. That was not what was happening here. The client didn't really say anything about anything but was just thinking aloud. Although I'm a huge enthusiast for sense making, it would have been fine for the client to have kept this in his head and declined to ask any questions.

But, within a minute of the exchange, the emboldened client continued, making declarative summary statements about the utility of a specific type of online tool. His descent into lecture mode was complete; he was not asking questions, but instead was sharing his own beliefs. He had transformed from a listener to a teller.

> **NOTE** LEARNING FROM MISTAKES
>
> I'm really beating up on "clients" a lot here! But there is no anti-client subtext at all; when you team up expert interviewers (my team) and novices (our clients) you get a glorious supply of illustrative examples. These examples remind me not to do these things; I'm using them to tell you not to do these things, and for both of us to coach our respective clients not to do these things either!

If You Have to Fix Something, Wait Until the End

If you are interviewing someone about your product, it will be tempting to help her have the best experience possible. You will invariably watch her struggle to find features, express a desire for something that you know is available, or hear her describe aspects of the product incorrectly. This can be very trying for an interviewer who is also passionate about the product. (Of course you are! After all, you are out in the field meeting customers in order to make the product better!) So how do you deal with this?

Do not jump in and correct or instruct her. This is just like the TiVo example, only more so! You are conducting the interview to learn from this person, so there's no need to assert your own expertise. In fact, once you do so, you can lose control over the interview entirely, as the participant will simply turn it around and ask you, "Is there a way to do_____? How can I make _____ happen?" Suddenly, your field visit has turned into the world's most expensive tech support house call.

By all means, at the end of the interview, as you are handing over the incentive and packing up, take a moment to share anything that you think might help that person. But ask yourself if explaining something is better for you or better for her. Don't correct her perceptions or terminology if the only outcome is "educating" her. Advocate for her, not for your product.

I led an interview with a fascinating professional who blew our minds with his insights into building up a professional network over decades of his career. As he was showing us how he worked, we saw him complain as he struggled to move the cursor between his two monitors, as the one on the left was set in Windows to be on the right. After we were finished, I offered to fix this, since it was something that came up peripherally in discussion. He was absolutely thrilled and quipped that this bit of support (even more than the incentive, or the tips my clients had given him about how to use their product) made the whole time worthwhile! Hyperbole or not, I was glad to be able to do something nice for him after he had been so wonderful to us.

Summary

When you're out in the field, actually doing your interview, keep the following in mind:

- Your field guide is a *guide*. Set it aside until you really need it. Leading the interview successfully comes down to *you*.

- Although it's tricky, ask the shortest question you can, without directing them to possible answers you are looking for. Then be silent.

- When you move from one topic to another, use transitional phrases such as "Great, I'd like to shift directions now...." or "Let's go back to something you said before...."

- Pay attention to whether or not you have received an answer to your question. Be prepared to follow up multiple times using different types of questions.

- Reflect back the language and terminology that your participant used (even if you think it was "wrong").

- If you want to fix something (say, a setting on their software) for your participant, wait until the interview is over.

CHAPTER 7

Documenting the Interview

O n one level, documentation is how you capture the definitive, fully detailed record of the interview (the "data"). On another level, it's how you, as the interviewer, make the ah-has and other important take-aways stick. While doing this, you have to stay engaged with the participant. Beyond that, documentation also bleeds into the sense making and storytelling that follow fieldwork.

Taking Notes

Although you might be tempted to try, you simply can't catch everything by taking notes. Typical handwriting is about 30 words per minute, and a great typist can do 60 wpm. Audio books are at least 100 wpm (and likely closer to 150 wpm). But people speak less clearly—and more quickly—than in an audio book. The cold math tells us it's just not possible to get everything down. Add the high cognitive load of leading an interview (as I talked about in the previous chapter), and you're done for. As transcriptionist Jo Ann Wall puts it, "It can be a challenge to listen purposefully in order to determine matters of importance and screen out extraneous information."

You do need to get *everything*. In the moment, you will miss details, misconstrue intent, or mishear a word. It's important to have an accurate version of the interview to go back to. The bottom line is that you should be recording your interviews—something I talk more about in more detail later in this chapter.

While I prefer to focus entirely on my interaction with the participant, some people find that taking notes helps them filter, synthesize, and ultimately better remember what is being discussed. The act of writing notes helps them process what is happening. They come away from the interview with pages and pages of handwritten rough notes. If you do this, remember that you must maintain eye contact while writing. Don't rely too heavily on asking your participants to wait while you catch up with what they've said. Worse still, you don't want to evoke the clichéd therapist who is bent into her notebook, muttering "mmm-hmm" and never looks up. By the same token, avoid overly signaling what you are interested in by scribbling furiously in response to certain types of input or response.

If, like me, you don't benefit from the act of note taking, you can assign this task to another researcher who joins you (or even a third party who is simply tasked with documentation). As you include other forms of documentation, you can easily become overwhelmed with devices and tasks outside leading the interview itself, so consider what can be assigned to a supporting interviewer.

As mentioned in the previous chapter, you can also take notes about what you want to remember during the interview, as a way to manage the expanding tree of the interview, as well as jot down topics you want to come back to.

NOTE (MIS)INTERPRETATIONS IN THE MOMENT

In one interview, I asked a participant, "If you and your wife own one iPod, how do you determine who is going to use it?" He responded, "Well, for commuting, it's either the iPod or the New Yorker." Two different scenarios are likely—1. She takes the iPod on the train, and he drives the car, a New Yorker, or 2. Whoever takes the iPod gets to listen to music, and the spouse gets to read the most recent issue of the *New Yorker* magazine. I didn't get to ask a clarification question, and it wasn't until I went back to the video that it was clear that he was referring to the magazine. In that same session, the participant, talking about iPods and design told us, "Well, when you do that, it looks more Zen. It actually looks like the competition" and another participant added, "Yes, it's like he says, very Zen, very Japanese, very spiritual." But that's not what the first participant meant by "Zen." He was referring to another MP3 player that was around at the time, called the Creative Zen. Misinterpretations in the moment are inevitable, so you need proper documentation to resolve it later.

Typing vs. Writing Your Notes

Many people can type faster than they can write. Typed notes can easily be shared electronically, and no one has to read your handwriting or interpret your spelling errors. However, taking notes on a computer creates other challenges. Do you have sufficient battery power or will you have to plug in? Can you type without clackety-clacking? What if you move around in the environment? Can you quickly move your laptop and still type on whatever surface is at hand? Can you continue to appear engaged even as you glance back and forth at the screen? Although this is also an issue when writing notes by hand, breaking eye contact to look at a screen can appear to be more rude (as participants wonder if you are checking email), while the screen itself can be more distracting for you.

Tablets and smartphones offer an alternative: although you won't be seen hiding behind the screen or lid, looking at a mobile device during the interview can be even more fraught with faux pas. It's not impossible to work around this issue, but simply showing up and using your smartphone as if you were in a meeting or on a date isn't going to cut it. Throw in the lower typing speeds, and you're limited in what you can do with these.

It's a good bet that interviewers who use note taking to help remember the interview are doing some kinesthetic learning; perhaps that effect isn't quite as strong when typing. If your goal is to juice your own memory, stick with writing. If you want roughs of the interview that can be shared (and you can keep your device interactions on the down-low), then type. And if you live for the moment, set it all aside and just focus on your interactions with your participant. Regardless, make sure that you are recording the entire interview using audio or video, as I discuss later in this chapter.

NOTE LIVESCRIBE SMARTPEN

LiveScribe makes something called a *smartpen*, which is a pen that records both audio and handwritten text (using special paper). After an interview, you can play back the audio from a certain portion of the interview by tapping on the relevant spot in your notes. Researchers who like taking notes find it generally unobtrusive and effective. Since I'm not an active notetaker, it's probably not a solution for me, but ethnographer Tricia Wang documents her evolving experience with her LiveScribe at **http://rfld.me/ZunZGi**.

The Notetaker's Voice

When taking notes, you should be descriptive, not interpretive. If Larry tells you he has worked 14 hours a day for the last 10 years, your notes should read "Worked 14 hrs/day for 10 years," not "Larry is a workaholic." If it's crucial to capture your interpretations, be sure to separate them from your observations, using capitalization or some other visual cue, such as "IS LARRY A WORKAHOLIC?" At this stage of rough notes, it's easy to lose track of what you were told versus the conclusions you made, so take care in how you document the two.

Audio Recording the Interview

An audio recording will capture all the verbal interactions between you and your participants. Of course, you can't see the demonstrations or exercises. Something like "I'd probably put this one with that one because they're kinda the same" might be hard to interpret later if you don't remember which items were being discussed. Although you can facilitate the discussion for the benefit of the audio recording (narrating what the participant is doing, like "So you would put the blue prototype in the same group as the orange prototype?"), it can feel unnatural. You shouldn't be treating the documentation as more important than the interpersonal interaction.

Depending on the environment, you can probably get away with a simple digital audio recorder. They are small and hold hours and hours of audio. Some background noise—especially clattering dishes and background music—can appear more prominent in the recording than you experience it, so perform some tests. Be aware of how loud you and your participant will sound in the final recording.

You might want to add an external mic to your audio recorder; think about whether it will allow you to move around the environment and whether it will pick up audio from multiple directions (at the very least, there's you and your respondent). Especially for the audio-tech newbie, I don't recommend a body microphone—everyone will have to be mic'd, and often a new participant will join spontaneously, different mics need to be mixed, and so on. The biggest concern is that attaching a body microphone is an intimate act that needs to happen at the beginning of the interview. When your relationship with the participant is at its most vulnerable, they will need to—with your guidance—attach a small device to their clothing, near their face. This is a delicate interaction that doesn't seem necessary if you can be satisfied with the audio quality.

You can also use a recording app in your smartphone, but test it first. Does your phone have enough capacity? What happens if a call comes in? Will your batteries last? And are you able to easily monitor the recording status of the app? There's nothing worse than realizing that your recording device has not actually been recording for the past half hour!

TIP TRANSCRIBING YOUR AUDIO FILES

You can get transcripts of your audio files (or even of the audio track of your video files). There are many transcription services that will take digital files via FTP (as they may be too large to email) and email back Word documents a few days later. Most services can remove "ummm..." and other hesitations and repeated words. This is called a "clean verbatim" transcript. I prefer to have those bits and pieces included because they help make the transcription come alive, revealing the personality of the respondent as well as illustrating the thinking process that goes into answering questions. I think this sort of human metadata is helpful in interpretation and analysis.

Costs for transcription depend on the total number of voices (how many interviewers and how many participants) as well as other typical factors like turnaround time, but you can expect to pay between $1.50 to $2.00 per minute.

by Ted Frank

Ted Frank is a storyteller with Backstories Studio. He has been in marketing for over 20 years and in consumer insights and strategy for more than 10.

As a company that has created hundreds of videos for research and strategy firms, Backstories Studio has seen too many examples of stellar research work become unusable because of poor video or sound quality. And it breaks our hearts. What's more, for some clients, the video deliverable is often the only way they see your insights. So it often becomes the way they evaluate you as well.

FIGURE 7.1
Ted Frank, Storyteller,
Backstories Studio

Here are some tips to get high-quality video, even if you have only five minutes to set up and have never been to film school:

- **Respondent placement:** Where you place your respondents is the biggest key to getting good quality. Pick a space that is quiet and bright enough to see the color of your respondent's eyes. And unless it's important to the project, select a place where the background does not distract from your respondent.

- **Light:** People tend to look best when light comes from the side and slightly in front of them (up to a 45° angle). A window works great in the daytime. Lights will work at night. Don't place your respondents with the window behind them, or they will appear dark. Lights shining down will light them, but they will appear older because of the shadows those lights create. Lighting them from the front will also work, but they can end up looking like an episode of *Cops*, and if light is in their eyes, it will make it difficult for them to see you. See Figure 7.2 for an optimal setup.

- **Sound:** In research, sound quality is often even more important than picture quality, especially if you're picking clips by what your respondents say. Where you place your microphone is everything. It's just like real life: People sound intimate when they're close to you and can be hard to hear when they're across the street. Shotgun mics work well for groups if you can point them at the person speaking. Because that's difficult, though, a second mic in the center of the group will save you. A lot of researchers get scared when they see that some of these mics can cost $400. However, if you rely on your camera mic alone, you'll end up paying that same money in editing costs to reduce the room noise. And your clip will still never sound as good as it would have if you placed the mic closer to your respondent to begin with. So it's better to spend the money initially and let your work shine.

- **Setting up the camera:** Thankfully, cameras have gotten a lot better over the years. An HD camera is a lot more affordable and will give your editor many more options for your final video. When setting up your camera, place it in front of your respondent, with the moderator in between it and the light or window (refer to Figure 7.2). It works best if the respondent is framed a bit to one side and looking across the frame, toward the moderator. When respondents look directly into the camera, the setting appears staged.

Frame your picture close if you want to capture emotion, but leave room in case your subject shifts or sways (and he always does). That will also leave you room for a nametag if you choose to place one in your video. Finally, look again at your respondent's eyes. If you can't see the color, move the light closer until you can.

Practice a few times before you get into field, and you'll be able to set all this up in just a few minutes. You'll end up with impressive video, and a lot fewer hours and expenses down the line.

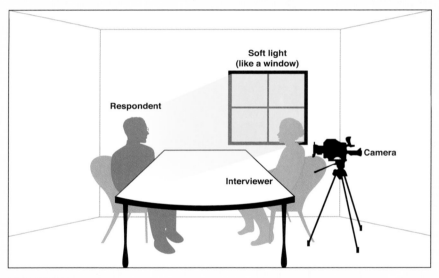

FIGURE 7.2
An optimal setup for placing the camera.

Video Recording the Interview

Video cameras are small, unobtrusive, and make for a viable default recording device. I take audio recorders as backup, but rely on video in most situations. With a video camera, you can capture the specifics of what the participant means by, "That part right there is the best one to use." You also can capture body language and nuanced elements in the conversation, which, of course, is not possible with audio recordings.

Buy an inexpensive mini (or "tabletop") tripod. This will make it easier to set the camera down during stationary parts of the interview, but will still allow you to easily grab it when you move around the environment. I haven't found that the presence of the camera is intimidating for people (especially in a post-YouTube era where it's a medium that we are all generally more familiar with), but setting it and forgetting it helps to focus you on the participant and the interview, rather than on the camera. When you are holding the camera, be aware that, even when it's facing away from you, the microphone is much closer to your mouth than the participant's, so be sensitive to your interjections, snickers, and mm-hmms, as they will really pop on the audio. For the novice interviewer, don't worry about moderating your rapport building for the camera, but for everyone else, it's worth keeping in mind.

> **TIP DON'T RUN OUT OF JUICE!**
>
> Be sure to have enough batteries on hand to get through the interview. I've found that cameras ship with a fairly small battery, but larger-capacity batteries are available, including compatible ones from third-party manufacturers. Shop online and stock up.

Although some cameras can adjust for backlighting, you should generally avoid having your participants in front of a window; even if you can see them, they will probably just appear in silhouette on the video.

Be prepared to manage the large files you create. Even on the lowest-quality settings, over the course of a small study you can end up with 20GB of video without trying too hard. That much digital data can fill up drives and is almost impossible for mortals (those of us with non-Pixar quality infrastructure) to move around a network.

Even if we don't edit video into a specific deliverable, it's often the richest archival artifact of the fieldwork. Video also reassures our clients that they can go back at any time to watch the interviews.

Photographing the Interview

Even if you're capturing imagery using video, still pictures are essential. When you make the deliberate choice to point and shoot, you are building the story of your participant. Even if the image in the camera is similar to a frame of video, that frame is packed in with all the other frames of video and requires effort for you to extract. You can return from the field with a set of photos and easily share an impromptu narrative of the interview by flipping through the photos on the camera. Even better, you will notice details in the photo that you didn't consciously perceive at the time. Video, with its audio track and its movement through time, doesn't as easily afford that extra detail. You might choose to just take still pictures and record audio and not bother recording video.

Be aware of how your picture taking will feel to the participants. Even though they agree to the use of photography when they sign your release, let the interview settle in before you start taking pictures. You can verbally confirm that it's okay before you take your first picture. If you are taking pictures of people, do it without the flash. If your second interviewer is taking pictures, they should not distract from the interview.

As I mentioned in Chapter 3, prepare a shot list so you have some ideas about which pictures you need to take.

Sketching the Interview

Sketching can be an appropriate medium when you can't take pictures. If you can't get an image of the participant's online banking screen, you can sketch the different regions of the interface and write callouts for some of his comments. Because he can see the sketch, he can be reassured that you aren't capturing private information and can clarify and correct your notes.

Caroline James takes that even further, using sketching as an active method to reflect back to her participants what she's hearing and to draw them out further (see Figure 7.3). She uses a combination of several specific techniques: visual recording, mind mapping, and visual note taking (sometimes referred to as "sketch noting").[1] She sketches in front of (and even with) her interview participants to engage them in creating a visual document of the interview.

I worked in the field with designer Jorge Gordon. His technique for note taking lay somewhere in between purely visual and purely textual; he used only words and lines but created a visual flow that captured his own experience (see Figure 7.4). As with many aspects of interviewing users, note taking can be highly individualistic.

> **TIP** COLLECTING ARTIFACTS
>
> Collect tangible examples from your fieldwork experience—buy an item from the company store, ask for a brochure, save your security pass, or keep the sample printout. These artifacts can go up on the wall in your analysis room, be passed around in meetings, or referred to later for inspiration, validation, or further insight.

---

1 A great intro is at http://rfld.me/QQ1Soj; also check out resources at http://rfld.me/1b6Zxo8.

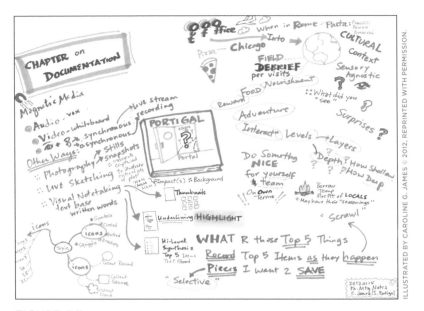

FIGURE 7.3
Caroline James took these notes while interviewing me about this chapter.

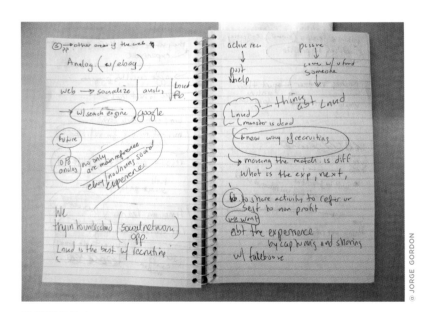

FIGURE 7.4
Jorge Gordon's fieldwork notes that include both sketch and text elements.

Debriefing After the Interview

When putting together your fieldwork schedule, you must absolutely allow time for debriefing after each interview. After you leave the fieldwork site, go for food and drink and talk about the interview. The longer you wait (say, until the next day or the next week), the less you will remember, and the more jumbled up the different interviews will become.

If you debrief as an open-ended conversation, make sure that someone takes notes (and shares them with everyone). Otherwise, use a debrief worksheet (see Figure 7.5) to capture initial thoughts, surprises, and changes for subsequent interviews. Ask, "What would we design for *this* user?" Don't worry about being too conclusive; this is a provocative way to start making sense of the interview. You aren't making design decisions; this is hypothetical, speculative, and easily discarded when future data takes you in a different direction. Make sure that your fellow researchers understand hypothesizing conclusions as a creative exercise.

Portigal Consulting LLC
415.894.2001
2311 Palmetto Ave., Suite D1
Pacifica, CA 94044

Portigal consulting

Debriefing Guide

participant: ________________ **researchers:** ________________ and ________________

Fill this out immediately after the interview, together with both interviewers. This document will serve as a key resource for the collaborative fieldwork debrief and analysis so please be thoughtful and thorough.

GETTING TO KNOW YOU-- *describe*

Describe the person we spoke to. What do they do? What are they into? What is their home environment like?

How did they describe their process of getting DEVICE?

LIFE WITH DEVICE

How are they using the DEVICE? What features are they using? What does this device mean to them?

What kinds of accessories do they use? Which ones aren't they using? Why?

What do they like most about the DEVICE? How is it best serving their needs?

What challenges have they had? What are some of their unmet needs and wishes?

What surprised them? What surprised you?

FIGURE 7.5
Sample debrief worksheet. See more at http://rfld.me/QLhHzy and http://rfld.me/UJkyHA.

Taking Field Notes

Many researchers sit down shortly after the interview and write up notes in some detail, using their notes, memory, and recordings. These field notes can easily run several pages long and emphasize narrative and description over conclusions or business implications. This is a time-consuming task and something I've stopped doing, especially since I began using transcripts. For trained social scientists, this is likely part of their training and an essential part of their process; while it is undoubtedly valuable, consider whether you have time in your schedule to do this.

Sample Field Highlights

by Kristine Ng, for the Omni Project[2]

The Elway family is composed of Arthur (dad), mom, and three kids (ages 13, 10, and 7). They recently moved to City 1 from City 2 and didn't have Internet for a month, which the kids thought was dreadful.

Arthur and two kids—Denise and Hayley—took part in the interview. Denise has a Kindle Fire, iPod, iHome, and cell phone. She really wanted a Nook, but her father persuaded her otherwise, since B&N isn't a tech company. She said she's tired of Apple products. She FaceTimes with her friends instead of talking on the phone, and sometimes texts them. Hayley has a first-gen iPad and iPod. She's eagerly waiting until she's old enough to get a cell phone. She's been promised one in February when she starts soccer, more as a means of communication with parents for rides and so on.

Regulating device use is a main concern for the family. Denise lost access to the Kindle as a punishment for misuse. Dad said that when they're doing homework they're only allowed to listen to music, but the girls have been caught FaceTiming and watching TV while doing homework. Arthur is interested in a solution for regulating these multi-use devices since part of their use is educational. He mentioned that City 2 is more affluent and the peer pressure is greater. There are second graders with cell phones (he doesn't think they need them) and 13-year-old girls with 10 pairs of Uggs. They're constantly trying to determine how to hold onto their values while understanding that peer pressure is real. Both parents closed their Facebook accounts, partially to be good role models, but her father also has privacy concerns. He would love to know what the best practices and guidelines are for device regulation.

---

2 A study about the impact that digital technology is having on our lives. See www.portigal.com/blog/announcing-the-omni-project/ for more info.

Sharing Field Highlights

As soon as possible after an interview, I write a rapid top-of-mind version of the session. I am not focused on capturing all the details but am creating a sharable story that brings a bit of the flavor of the fieldwork to the broader team. With practice, these highlights (which I affectionately refer to as "quickies") take only a few minutes to write and email. Some of the effort to produce these highlights is in restraining yourself from trying to produce field notes. See an example of field highlights in Kristine Ng's sidebar on p. 116.

Summary

By documenting the interview, you are capturing a definitive detailed record of the interview. It's also a way for you to process and remember the insights and take-aways that come to you while the interview is happening.

- You can't catch everything by taking notes. You do need to get *everything*. In the moment, you will miss details or mishear a word.

- Recording audio or video is the only way to capture all the details of your interview.

- If you take notes on a computer or other device, can you do so silently and maintain your engaged eye contact with the participant?

- Notes should be descriptive rather than interpretive; when you go back to them later, it's hard to tell the difference between what actually happened and your own interpretations.

- Use a small video camera with a pocket tripod or a simple digital audio recorder; external mics will improve audio quality, but body mics create an awkward interaction with the participant when setting up.

- Have plenty of batteries for all of your devices and be aware of how long they should last.

- Take lots of pictures; they often reveal something different later on.

- Sit down with the field team right after the interview and debrief about key take-aways. Soon after, write up quick highlights and share them with the rest of your team.

CHAPTER 8

Optimizing the Interview

An interview is an interaction between two humans. Or throw in a colleague and a spouse, and now it's an interaction between four humans—irrational, emotional, language-using, unpredictable humans. The only one of these four you have any control over is yourself. This is a messy business. There will always be variables and curve balls. This chapter looks at some of the more common challenges that you will face in the field. It also suggests a number of ways to develop your own skills so that you are prepared for future surprises.

Troubleshooting Common Interview Problems

Many of the situations discussed in this section stem from something that happened leading up to the interview, such as how the participants were recruited. The best troubleshooting approach is to prevent these problems from occurring through proper screening and clear setting of expectations. Realistically, though, they will still come up.

When the Participant Is Reticent

Are you sure that your participant is holding back? As discussed in Chapter 6, his default demeanor and speaking rhythm may simply be out of sync with yours.

If you conclude that he is indeed uncomfortable, try to identify the cause and make a change in the way you are handling the interview. You might simply need to accept the awkwardness and be patient with yourself and with him, looking toward a point where he becomes more comfortable. If he is connecting better with one of your colleagues, ask that person to lead the rest of the interview. If there are too many interviewers, ask one of them to step back. If you aren't giving your participant enough verbal space to reflect and respond, slow down and let him talk. If your participant needs more structure, fall back to straightforward, direct questions.

Consider which aspects of your topic might be making him uncomfortable. Even if an interview doesn't explore social taboos, you may be tapping into an element of personal insecurity about his job, his competence, his intelligence, and so on. Or you can change the topic, share your enthusiasm for his talent, or reveal something about yourself.

Sometimes you might find yourself in a different situation than you had anticipated. For example, an interview with a certain type of professional turns out to be an interview with that person *and* his manager. If you can't get the interview you want (perhaps by gently suggesting you interview them each separately), be aware of the dynamics and adjust your questions appropriately. Ask the manager questions about herself or about her understanding of how the work is performed.

If all else fails, consider asking your participant outright to identify the source of his discomfort. Tell the participant that this information is important to you and your work and that you are deeply interested, but you are concerned that he isn't comfortable with the conversation. Ask what would be better, even if it means a different time or a different location.

When the Participant Isn't the Right Kind of User

Assuming you've screened your subject, you might wonder how that person can end up being wrong for the study. If you are surprised—or even uncomfortable—at how reality differs from what you expected, that's a crucial insight. But don't be hasty to dismiss the participant.

If you've taken the time to travel to this participant's home or workplace, you should complete the interview. Consider what you might do with the 45 minutes you could save by cutting out early and how that stacks up against the possibility that you might learn something by interviewing this person about his experience and perspective. Reset your expectations and see what you can get out of the session. Afterward, revisit your screening criteria. You may have uncovered the fact that a word or phrase in the criteria is being interpreted differently by participants (for example, "late-model car" could mean one thing to your team and another to the people you are recruiting). Also, if you have identified additional factors for the rest of the participants, you might want to rescreen them.

> **NOTE** GETTING THE RIGHT PARTICIPANT
> AND THE RIGHT CONTEXT
>
> In several studies, I recruited participants who were users of various devices (like laptops, video cameras, and MP3 players). They had told us they owned these devices and used them for whatever tasks we were interested in. But several times I found myself at the interview, discovering that the device in question wasn't actually at their home, where the interview was conducted. One person worked for an airline and had homes in two cities. Another person met us at his girlfriend's house, where none of his stuff was located. Another lived with roommates and her young children, while her computer was at the home of their father. And so on. After this happened a few times, I updated the language of my screener to ensure that the interview would take place in their primary residence and where the device was, and that they would be prepared to show us the device during the interview.
>
> During another project, we were seeking people who were actively sharing certain types of information. One participant was indeed actively sharing this information, but only with his

immediate family, with whom he lived some of the time. We hadn't specified that "sharing" should take place with a broader network, and even though we had reviewed the screener with our client, no one had seen this as a concern. From this interview, it emerged that we all had different ideas of what "sharing" meant. Our client was very concerned since they had conceived of sharing as a different behavior. In the interview itself, we focused on learning everything we could from this participant, but in the aftermath we had a number of intense conversations with the client to determine whether or not this participant was acceptable for the study.

When the Participant Won't Stop Talking

As you settle into a rhythm with participants, you may realize that they talk extensively, requiring little or no prompting from you. Before you try to "fix" this issue, ask yourself whether this really is a problem. You have prepared extensively and have a lot of questions you're hoping to ask, but are you getting what you need from this participant? If you don't feel in control, you might be annoyed, but keep the emotional factor separate and assess the interview in terms of the information you need. In some cases, they won't be answering your questions at all. Give them space to tell the story they've chosen to tell you and then redirect them back to your question. For example, consider the following exchange, which is drawn from a real experience:

Q: What kind of food do you prepare for yourself?

A: When I was a child [long story about her mother, etc., etc.]

Q: So how does that experience as a child impact the decisions you make now for your family?

Your last resort is to interrupt. If you must interrupt, frame it appropriately—"Excuse me! I'm so sorry to interrupt, but I know we have a limited amount of time, and I want to make sure we cover the topics we're here to learn about."

NOTE CONFERENCE INTERRUPTUS

I was at a conference in Bangalore. The last session of the day included a fairly spirited Q&A. There were two microphones going around, and while an audience member and a panelist were going back and forth on one mic, I got the other. The discussion was degrading; the audience member was fixated on some issue and was not going to let it go, but there was no resolution. The conversation had devolved into posturing and deflection. People began to get annoyed and mutter and shift in their seats. They saw me with the microphone and began, quietly at first and then more insistently, to encourage me to interrupt. I could see that interrupting was within the norm for this culture, but even as I was standing up and being cheered on, it was extremely difficult for me to interrupt. I succeeded in opening my mouth, but nothing came out. Twice. Meanwhile, the droning, time-wasting back-and-forth continued, and my fellow attendees were losing patience with me. Finally, I was able to interrupt, but it was a significant challenge, even with all the affirmation! In an interview, I find interrupting just as difficult and do it only when I absolutely have to.

When You Feel Uncomfortable or Unsafe

Unless you are going to a public or familiar corporate location, don't conduct interviews on your own. When you arrive at a location, verify that everyone feels safe. Pay attention to the difference between *unsafe* and *uncomfortable*[1]. If you feel unsafe, don't go in. If you feel uncomfortable, try to set that feeling aside and proceed (see Figures 8.1 and 8.2).

FIGURE 8.1
Check your gut reaction. If you feel uncomfortable, it may still be okay to proceed.

---

1 See http://johnnyholland.org/2009/06/lets-embrace-open-mindedness/ (scroll down to the section entitled "Getting Out of the Comfort Zone") for some thoughts about acknowledging people's discomfort in new or different situations). Coming to grips with this discomfort is a wonderful way to grow as an interviewer.

FIGURE 8.2
If you feel unsafe, pay attention to that feeling and stay away from dangerous places.

There will be plenty of strange interviews. It's an hour or two of your life; if you aren't in danger, do your best to learn what you need to learn, acknowledge that life is interesting, and add the experience to your set of war stories.[2]

Women are unfortunately more likely to encounter awkwardness and comments that push the boundaries. If you feel increasing discomfort in response to someone else's behavior, take a moment to pause and identify what's happening. You might want to call for a bathroom break. If you are at risk, leave. Otherwise, you can ignore the behavior (but not the person) or restate your objectives and give the participant the opportunity to agree to continue with that focus. Of course, be aware of your own limits and be prepared to leave if the situation deteriorates.

---

2 Danger is a personally subjective issue. In this video https://vimeo.com/9217883, Luis Arnal describes his design-research adventures, including arranging with gang leaders to gain access to Brazilian slums (know as favelas) for fieldwork, the consequences of inadvertently photographing an FBI undercover operation, and (if not dangerous then perhaps uncomfortable) participating in one of Spencer Tunick's massive nude photo shoots.

After a long few days of fieldwork, my client and I headed to Los Angeles's Toy District to interview a wholesaler. Driving separately, we had each struggled naïvely through traffic the way that out-of-towners do and were searching for parking. I left my car in a no-parking spot and went to verify our meeting location. Our interview was with a small business owner. I was picturing a typical retail setting, with a familiar storefront, street numbers, etc. Instead, I found a street filled with stalls jammed with merchandise, with few prominent building numbers (many were just scrawled in marker on the outer edges of the stalls). Something about this did not feel right, so I called our recruiter and got confirmation that we were indeed in the right place.

I left my car in a lot and walked to meet my client, who was still in his car, circling. I got into his car and related my impressions as he navigated traffic, still looking for parking. The long days, the daunting traffic, the unfamiliar surroundings, and the parking problems had been accumulating until something within him snapped. He turned red, made a sudden turn, and floored the accelerator. Fortunately for me, his venting of emotions gave me space to be "the calm one" (although no doubt I had fed his anxiety with my own). We drove a few blocks, and I made some very concrete suggestions about where to park. Once calmness returned, we both could see that there was nothing really wrong, but we had just reached the end of our ropes. We got some food and walked back to our interview. We were overwhelmed and exhausted, and the lack of familiarity caused a brief and intense descent into fear. That experience with the fight-or-flight reflex helped me more finely parse the difference between discomfort and danger.

Interview Variations and Special Cases

While I've devoted much of this book to the optimal case where you and your participant have arranged the best possible interview situation, there are inevitably exceptions. In this section, I'll look at how to deal with some of these situations:

- You and your participant are not in the same location.

- You meet your participant in a neutral location, out of his context.

- You have only a short amount of time for the interview.

- You are interviewing people as "professionals" rather than as "consumers."

- You have multiple participants in a single interview.

When Your Interview Isn't Face-to-Face

Phone interviews are a fairly common alternative to face-to-face interviews, especially when geographic distance makes a face-to-face interview unrealistic. Since you won't have as much context (see Figure 8.3), look for other ways to compensate. Ask participants beforehand to send some digital photos of their environment or to describe elements you won't be able to see during the call. When arranging the interview, establish their expected location. (For example, will they be in their car in traffic, or will they be at home caring for their children?) At the same time, confirm the length of the interview. For most people, an hour is a long time to be on the phone.

During a phone interview, a lack of facial cues makes it a bit harder to adjust your pace and rhythm to the participant. Experiment with giving your participant an extra beat of silence to ensure she feels permitted to speak, and to allow her to continue to speak. If silence is making her uncomfortable (you get a, "Hello? Are you there?"), pick up the pace a bit and introduce verbal handoffs (such as, "Go ahead...please continue...").

If you use technologies like Skype (for audio or video) and FaceTime, you are introducing other complicating factors:

- Your participant might not be fully proficient at using these tools. It's not ideal to begin the interview having your participant exasperated and feeling incompetent.

- You are subject to the variability of Internet connection speeds (and software reliability) on both ends. Four minutes of reconnecting and dropping calls is not acceptable, so arrange for a technology test before the interview.

FIGURE 8.3
When the interviewer and participant can't see each other, it's anyone's guess how their contexts differ.

- Not everyone is fully literate in video conferencing. Consider your audience. You might want to warm up the interview with a discussion of the communication context ("It's unfortunate we couldn't meet with you face-to-face. Do you regularly meet with people via Skype?").

When Your Interview Is in a Market Research Facility

Focus group companies offer meeting rooms designed for market research, with mirrored-wall observation rooms, video recording, and all the other accoutrements. It would be a mistake to consider these facilities as neutral third places. When you invite people to come to a facility to be interviewed, they are coming to *your* house. Unfortunately, all the comfy couches, Nerf balls, and tasty snacks don't change that. You must be the host instead of the guest. Even if you don't feel settled in this new environment yourself, you must welcome them into your space. You can ask them to bring something of theirs (photos, artifacts, or a collage) to the interview, but this approach is a definite compromise.

When Your Interview Is Very Short

If you can get only a short amount of time from people, warm them up ahead of time. Get them thinking about your topics by emailing them some key questions to think about. They don't need to write up their answers ahead of time; they can just be reflecting on these topics and be prepared to share some perspective. You won't have time to probe too much. Stick to the agreed-upon time unless they offer to talk longer, and then make an explicit request for a follow-up interview.

The Differences in Interviewing Professionals vs. Consumers

Consumer interviews will probably take place in the home. When interviewing professionals, you might find yourself on a trading floor, in a hospital, in a restaurant, in an office, in a manufacturing facility, or in any other kind of environment. Professionals might have to perform their work tasks intermittently or continuously as they are interviewed, so you might be doing bouts of passive observation, or you might be asking for narration of processes rather than exploring other topics. Depending on what you need to do when interviewing professionals, you need to be very specific in your interview request—duration, environment, role, and so on.

Consumers might default to treating your interview like a *visit*. Professionals often frame the interview as a *meeting*. You can choose to operate within those expectations, or you can seek to shift them, but keep in mind where your participant is coming from.

Interviewing Multiple Participants

We often ask other family members to join interviews, or we may speak to colleagues simultaneously when interviewing professionals. This is best when you aren't expecting power dynamics to significantly impact the interview (such as a subordinate being asked to explain his career goals in front of his boss; or a teen being asked about her alcohol consumption in front of her parents). If need be, you can break the interview into separate chunks for each participant individually and for the group together.

In terms of group dynamics, your goal should be to get the participants talking extemporaneously, even to each other. Do not conduct two parallel identical interrogations; instead, gently lead a conversation by throwing your questions open and using eye contact and specific probes directed at individuals to encourage them to contribute. As you hold back, they will step forward.

Instead of this:

Interviewer: When did you start drinking Kombucha?

P1: About six months ago.

Interviewer: How about you, when did you start drinking Kombucha?

P2: It was about four months ago.

Interviewer: And what is it about Kombucha that draws you to it?

P1: I like the taste.

Interviewer: What about you?

P2: I like the way I feel after.

Aim for this:

Interviewer: When did you each start drinking Kombucha?

P1: About six months ago.

Interviewer: [Pause]

P2: Oh, for me it was about four months ago.

Interviewer: And what is it about Kombucha?

P1: I like the taste.

P2: You do? I actually can't stand the taste but...I like the way I feel after.

P1: But tell them about what happened when you drank that tiny bottle last week!

You'll have more success with people who already know each other. As I mentioned earlier when considering the number of interviewers, people influence each other simply by being together.[3] The more people you include, the more you'll experience that effect.

Using Different Interviewing Techniques at Different Points in the Development Process

Regardless of your business objectives, you always want to understand how the participant makes sense of the world, and what problems and concerns they have. You may be early in the development process and have broad questions, or you may be further along and have hypotheses (concepts, animations, storyboards, designs, wireframes, and more). In the latter case, spend the first part of the interview understanding the participant's workflow, objectives, pain points, and so on. Then, when you share the artifacts you've brought, you have a better chance at understanding *why* they are responding the way they do. If you aren't interested in that amount of detail and just want reactions to your prototype, you're better off doing usability testing, not interviews.

Improving as an Interviewer

Now that you've learned some techniques for interviewing, you can hone and refine your performance further by practicing, reflecting, critiquing, collecting, and sharing.

Practice

Don't forget that interviewing is like any skill: the more you practice, the better you get. Even the busiest researcher only gets to do a certain number of interviews, so be creative in generating or finding other opportunities to practice. Take advantage of brief everyday encounters (say, that loquacious taxi driver) and do a little bit of interviewing, asking questions and follow-up questions. Cultivate a style of interacting socially that emphasizes listening, reflecting back the other person's comments, allowing for silence, and so on. Try for longer and deeper conversations to build up your stamina.

When you are in the field, remember that each interview is also a learning experience. Try something different once in a while. Use the interview guide from back to front while still maintaining rapport and keeping a comfortable flow; force yourself to count to five before everything you say; don't just take notes, take copious notes.

---

3 See http://en.wikipedia.org/wiki/Asch_conformity_experiments or http://en.wikipedia. org/wiki/Normative_social_influence for more.

Reflect

You can get the most out of any interview by reflecting on it. Football coaches review game films, and user researchers can do similarly. You have the material: audio, video, or transcripts. Otherwise, conduct and capture mock interviews specifically for this purpose. Look for moments that went well or moments that went slightly awry and think about what you would do differently. Don't beat yourself up about how you handled it in the moment; the benefit of reflection is that you can stop time and consider a range of options.

Seek out opportunities to be interviewed yourself. Although phone surveys or online customer satisfaction surveys use a different methodology, the participants aren't thinking about that; they are just being asked questions. Sign up for market research databases or volunteer for grad student studies. Go through the experience and notice when it feels bad (and anytime it feels right). You can use these insights to avoid, or replicate, such interview techniques.

Leverage your past experiences with strangers, such as going on blind dates, working as a bartender or waiter, being interviewed for a job, and more. What principles did you develop in those situations? Consider what worked and what didn't and why.

Critique

In addition to reviewing your own interviews, review other people's, too (and ask them to review yours). Tag along during interviews and watch someone's technique. Teach someone else how to lead an interview. Or ask someone to come along to your interviews and get his feedback. Also ask for feedback from the rest of your field team (even if you are the lead interviewer), or even from your research participants.

Check out interviews in the media: Terry Gross, Charlie Rose, Barbara Walters, Oprah Winfrey, and Marc Maron are good places to start (see Figure 8.4). Watch and listen as an interviewer, not just an audience member. Although the context of journalism (writ large) differs from user research, you will notice techniques both new and familiar.

FIGURE 8.4
Marc Maron is a comedian, not a journalist. His interviews (see Chapter 6) are a good source of both positive and negative examples.

And More

Collect and share your fieldwork *war stories*.[4] These experiences—the crazy household, the dog that does his business on your shoes, the GPS failure— are inevitable and are often hilarious (at least in hindsight). Exchanging these stories is a way of sharing techniques and creates learning opportunities for both the tellers and listeners.[5] A culture of exchange—wherever you can find it—is going to help you grow your own skills. You can check out (and contribute to) a growing archive of fieldwork war stories at www.portigal. com/series/WarStories.

---

4 As in this Merriam-Webster definition: "A recounting of a memorable personal experience, especially one involving challenge, hardship, danger, or other interesting features."

5 In Per Brandström's thesis *Boundless Universe: The Culture of Expansion Among the Sukuma-Nyamwezi of Tanzania,* he describes how anthropologists in the field often gather at a hotel bar and "release a torrent of stories about bizarre and remarkable happenings and experiences in exotic settings, and each anthropologist will try and top the others' wildest stories... When the laughter dies away and the entertainer is transformed into the scientist, a sudden change of scene has taken place. The anecdotes and the wild stories are stowed away. Now order is the rule of the day; facts and theories will be presented."

Take an improv class. Improv training helps develop many aspects of interviewing, such as being in the moment, holding back judgment, and listening.[6] Alternatively, meditation can help you be present during interviews and develop the mental energy it takes to focus deeply on someone else.

Connect with other interviewers online[7] and at conferences.[8] Read books about interviewing (Hey, you're doing that right now! Well done!) and about interpersonal communication.[9] As you learn more, you can identify your own personal style and adjust for it.

6 I've given a number of talks about improv in the context of design and design research. Video from one presentation is at www.ustream.tv/recorded/2595655 and the slides are at www.slideshare.net/steveportigal/yes-my-iguana-loves-to-chacha-improv-creativity-and-collaboration.

7 Try the anthrodesign group at http://tech.groups.yahoo.com/group/anthrodesign/.

8 In addition to design and UX conferences, check out ethnography conferences such as EPIC (www.epicconference.com).

9 For example, books by Deborah Tannen; see www9.georgetown.edu/faculty/tannend/.

Summary

Interviewing is made of people, and as such your experiences in the field will be unpredictable and surprising. Be prepared for what might go awry and how you will deal with it.

- If you feel your participant is reticent, be sure it's not just a difference between her speaking rhythm and yours. Try to identify what's making her uncomfortable and make adjustments. If necessary, ask about any possible discomfort. Or just accept the awkwardness and move forward until she opens up.

- You may not initially feel a participant is right for the study. Once you are there interviewing, stick with it. If he isn't what you expected (despite deliberate screening), that is something worth reflecting on later; meanwhile, what can you learn from him now?

- If you think your participant is talking too much, ask yourself if that's because you are feeling out of control or because you aren't getting the information you want. If you must interrupt, apologize and remind him that you value his limited time.

- In a phone interview, lack of visual cues makes it harder to adjust your pace and rhythm to the participant. Give her an extra beat and give yourself permission to feel awkward in those small moments of silence or overlap.

- If you have only a very brief amount of time for your interview, prime your participant ahead of time with some questions or topics you plan to discuss.

- When interviewing several people at once, avoid asking each person the same question in turn. Use eye contact to create a more free-flowing dialogue where some questions are addressed to an individual while others are thrown to the group. Allow them to follow-up each other's points and even ask each other questions.

- Be aware of the difference between discomfort and fearing for your safety. Develop a tolerance for the former but do not compromise on the latter.

- Improve your interviewing skills by practicing, varying from your habitual approach, reviewing transcripts and videos, and seeking critiques from others.

Making an Impact with Your Research

Although I've necessarily dwelled on the details of the interview, as the book comes to a close, it makes sense to step back and revisit why you're conducting the interviews. It's not only to learn about people, but also to take the information back to the organization in a way that it can be acted upon. You want to be sure that data becomes insights, and insights become opportunities—for new products, features, services, designs, and strategies, but also new opportunities for teams to embrace a user-centered approach to their work.

So what happens with all this great data? Although analysis and synthesis (not to mention design) easily merit their own books, in this chapter I'll provide an overview of a process you can use to sort through all your data.

Analyzing and Synthesizing Your Interview Data

Working with research data is a combination of *analysis*, or breaking larger pieces into smaller ones (for example, interviews and transcripts into anecdotes and stories) and *synthesis*, or combining multiple pieces into something new (for example, building themes, implications, and opportunities).

This combination of analysis and synthesis is part of the iterative process of working through the data. Although multiple iterations are beneficial, the two steps that are most important are:

- Informally processing the experiential data in your head from having conducted all the interviews

- More rigorously diving into the documented data (the notes, videos, photos, transcripts, and so on)

In Chapter 7, I described debriefs and field highlights. These are two ways that you begin the analysis and synthesis process during fieldwork. After you've finished gathering data, you should compile a starter set with anywhere from 5 to 15 thematic areas that build on these debriefs and highlights and address the research objectives. You may also have some clues about new patterns. At this stage, you're really only processing the experience of being in the field. Given that fact, it's appropriate to simply identify interesting areas and provocative questions, such as, "There seems to be a relationship between people's comfort with making mistakes and their use of different companies' productions." You don't need to know what the relationship actually is at this point; instead, you are just noting patterns and weak signals (a term from electrical engineering that has been adopted by futurists) that you see.

Create a Topline Report

This set of emerging themes and early findings becomes a *topline report.* See the example in the sidebar that follows. (You can see the whole report at http://rfld.me/UoGeOw.) Determine what provokes your client's interest (and where you might encounter skepticism) in order to bring focus to your next steps.

In the introduction to the topline, I included the following statements:

> Topline is based on early impressions, not formal analysis of data. This is a chance to share stories and initial insights from the fieldwork; to discuss what jumped out at us and list questions we still have.

An introduction like this helps set the expectations for the client team. My clients sometimes tell me they are afraid their colleagues will take early findings and dash off to implementation, so I work hard to clarify where we are in the process. I include key milestones from the overall project calendar where I can point to what is coming next, how future deliverables will be different than what's in the topline, and when they can expect them.

I create topline reports in Microsoft Word. A Word document is more formalized than an email but less formal than a PowerPoint presentation, and this is the balance I'm trying to strike. Ongoing dialogue is usually in email; the final presentation is in PowerPoint. This deliverable is right in the middle. I want enough formality that the appearance of the topline is appropriate to a milestone in the project (that's the conclusion of full-on fieldwork and the transition into full-on analysis and synthesis), but with enough looseness that the content isn't misinterpreted to be more conclusive or actionable than is warranted.

Deeply Processing Your Data

After the topline report comes the more formal data processing stage. This is important because this step is where you will uncover significant new insights that go well beyond the topline. You will get your data in text form and divide it among the team. This typically includes everyone who went in the field and optionally others who were available for this part of the process. But don't spread the data too thinly; people do best if they have at least two or three interviews to work with. Make sure that each interview has been assigned to a team member.

1. Reading is not just a solo activity; there are significant social/interpersonal aspects for many people.

- Recommendations, book clubs, lending

- Books facilitate the interpersonal aspects of reading:

    - Can be easily lent or given away

    - Can be given as gifts

    - People can use a book together: parents and kids, showing someone a passage or illustrations, and so on

- Reading can be a big part of family life

- Childhood memories, passing books between generations, reading with one's own children

- Connection between home life and outside world (school)

2. Reading and books are not always one and the same.

- Erica buys some books because she likes them as objects. She knows she might not read all of them. "I love books. I almost like books more than reading."

- Jeff says if you love to read, you'd like the Kindle. If you love books, you should try it out before you buy one.

- The Kindle facilitates types of reading beyond books: blogs, articles, and periodicals.

3. Books do more than carry content.

- Books engage the senses—they are tactile, visual objects, with specific characteristics like smell and weight.

    - They become carriers of specific memories

    - They develop a patina that carries meaning

    - An inscribed book becomes a record of an event, interaction, or relationship

---

1 A study about the future of reading and books. See www.portigal.com/blog/ reading-ahead-project-launch/ for more info.

- There is an art/collector aspect to books, which is absent on the Kindle.
    - First editions
    - Signed copies
    - Galley proofs
    - Typography
    - Pictures and illustrations
    - Quality of paper, printing, and so on
- Books say something about a person.
    - Others can see what you're reading; like clothes and other belongings, this carries meaning
    - "Looking at someone's bookshelves when you go to their house" (Jeff)
    - When people give books as gifts, they are deliberately communicating something about the relationship, the event, themselves, and the recipient
- Books can create a physical record of someone's reading activity.
    - Chris used to line up all the books he had read to get a sense of accomplishment
    - Annotations, bookmarks, and tags convey the reader's personal history with that book

4. Books are easily shared.
- Pass them along to others
- Donate to library
- Sell or buy at a used bookstore
- Borrow from the library rather than purchase

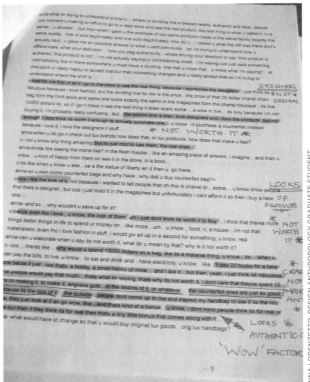

ANNA LORENZETTO, DESIGN ANTHROPOLOGY GRADUATE STUDENT, SWINBURNE UNIVERSITY OF TECHNOLOGY

FIGURE 9.1
A marked-up interview transcript showing a few different levels of annotation.

Each team member should go through his portion of the transcripts quickly, making short marginal notes on patterns, key quotes, or whatever seems interesting (see Figure 9.1). These notes can be in the form of labels ("This is another example of BLURRING BOUNDARIES"), questions ("Where did she get this process?"), or even hypothesized solutions ("They really need that all-in-one robot here!").

The group should then reconvene and present each interview as a case study. You can give a bit of background about the individual, and then page through your marginal notes and pick out the provocative highlights. Discuss each interview briefly, and then create a sticky note that summarizes the key point of that interview. Each case study will take about an hour on average. As you are accumulating stickies, take a few moments to create *groupings*. You may want to start with the categories from your topline and add to them. As you assemble those groupings, you will collectively begin to develop a new, shared point of view that goes beyond the mere findings.

FIGURE 9.2

In analysis/synthesis sessions, stories and examples from transcripts and other data are synthesized into key findings, takeaways, and opportunities.

A precise articulation of that point of view, including the implications for business and design, becomes the *Presentation of Findings*, which is the main research deliverable. The specifics will obviously depend on your research question as well as the makeup of your team and stakeholders.

The transcript of a two-hour interview might run 35 pages, and with a bit of practice in skimming and annotating, you can get through it in under an hour. Presenting the first few interviews to the group will take a very long time, because everything is new and everything is interesting. By the time you get to the end, you'll be moving much more quickly. Plan for a series of 3–4 hour sessions (see Figure 9.2) and expect to average about an hour per interview. Of course, there are more opportunities for synthesis as you transform your results into some form of deliverable.

Research as a Leadership Activity

When I give seminars or workshops about the methods and techniques you've been reading about in this book, I'm frequently asked to address the challenges facing people who are not only interested in learning these methods but also are passionate about advocating for this approach. The best practices outlined in this section are based on what I've seen my clients do, as well as insights I've gleaned from interviews with a number of thought leaders working inside large organizations in industry.

Championing the Use of Research in Your Organization

You should position yourself in your organization so that interviewing customers is an integral part of how you work. If this wasn't part of your arrangement upon being hired, you need to evolve your brand with your managers and colleagues. If you can't do that, consider your future in that organization. If your values are not aligned, ask yourself how feasible it is to shift their values versus finding another job where your approach is welcomed.

If your employer has a fast-follower strategy, your plan to use insights to drive breakthrough offerings is unlikely to succeed. Look at Jess McMullin's Design Maturity Model in Figure 9.3 and identify where your organization is today (and where it's going). You might suggest, for example, that in order to do something new in the market, you have to do something new with your process, but if management doesn't want to do something new in the market, your argument will fall on deaf ears.

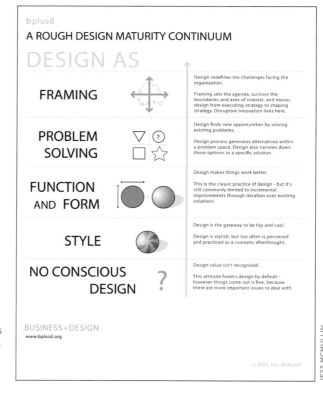

FIGURE 9.3
A model that illustrates the progression of how organizations think of and utilize design.

Identify allies who will advocate for the kind of research you want to do. You may find newly hired leaders who believe in certain best practices from previous jobs, or isolated designers and researchers elsewhere in the corporation who are looking for their own peers and champions, or managers who know there must be a better way to reach users but don't know where to start. Reach out to the professional community for mentors, inspiration, and peer support, and to benchmark your successes against others.

If you are getting pushback about interviewing users, identify the objection and target your proposal accordingly. If you're being told that the team already knows what they need to design, is that true? If so, why haven't previous initiatives succeeded? Take time to understand the problem you are being asked to solve. What has already been tried? What worked and what didn't work? Base your recommendations on that context. You aren't asking for permission here; you are making a case for solving their problem.

If there is concern about resources, be aware of what it takes to do this sort of research (see Figure 9.4 for a typical timeline), and if you want to tighten the deadlines, be aware—and make sure your stakeholders are aware—of the trade-offs of doing so (see Figure 9.5). Sometimes resistance to committing resources is based on naïve assumptions about what is necessary (such as, "We have to see every type of customer."). Your expertise in project planning will help scope the project appropriately. Determine the research needs and propose the right size project that will address them, highlighting costs and trade-offs.

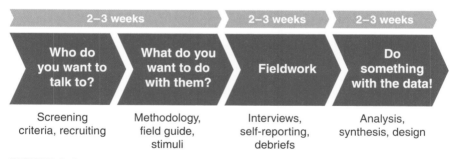

FIGURE 9.4
Timeframe for a typical project interviewing users.

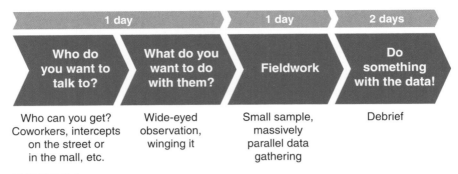

1 day	1 day	2 days
Who do you want to talk to?	**What do you want to do with them?**	**Fieldwork**	**Do something with the data!**

Who can you get? Coworkers, intercepts on the street or in the mall, etc.

Wide-eyed observation, winging it

Small sample, massively parallel data gathering

Debrief

FIGURE 9.5
Working with tighter deadlines means making trade-offs.

Help your organization understand that interviewing users is a special skill, beyond the general process of "talking to people." Training, delivered by you or by an external specialist, will reveal user research as a special skill, and will empower more people to go out and interview users. You shouldn't just be looking for opportunities to do user research yourself; you should be trying to get the company to embrace this overall approach. When partnering with external research vendors, highlight their relevant expertise (mobile, teen media consumption, medical, and so on).

Be proactive in identifying opportunities to learn about users. Instead of waiting for requests (which are likely to be more tactical than strategic), look for design questions and business questions and propose research that will serve multiple teams and initiatives.

For example, when a client repeatedly approached me with requests for proposals on similar studies ("How are tech-forward individuals managing their digital music?" "How are tech-forward households streaming media between devices?" "How are tech-forward people using mobile?"), I suggested an alternative approach, investigating instead their "digital daily lives." This proposal went all the way to the CEO, who was reportedly excited about it, but then instead reorganized their design, research, and innovation teams. While the consulting project never materialized, I believe we helped catalyze an overdue discussion about team structure and process.

Maximizing Research Impact

To maximize the impact of the research you do, be sure to engage the organization throughout the process, from setting the research agenda, to the detailed planning and joining you in the field. Members of the organization can be involved in the analysis and synthesis activities, from the topline through reading transcripts and identifying patterns and themes.

The most impact for the least effort comes from your colleagues joining you in the field. When managed properly (see Chapter 5, "Key Stages of the Interview"), even a single interview can show individuals that how the organization has been thinking about user needs is incomplete. For some teams, this engagement is ultimately more powerful than any traditional research output. Creating alignment and revising entrenched belief structures are two higher-order benefits that come from research. They help position user research as an essential strategic tool.

Make your process visible. When a client couldn't get a meeting room for a massive fieldwork debriefing, he took over the kitchen area. Many people walked by and peeked in, intrigued, to see what was happening.

Articulate research findings in ways that are most relevant to your stake-holders. Will you have the most impact by telling stories, defining needs, specifying requirements, or producing prototypes? One research team realized that results like "Users need it to be easy to clean" were not actionable by their internal customers. They evolved their process to articulate specifically what the engineers should do, with recommendations like "Surfaces should be made from elastomeric materials and all joining pieces should have no more than a 1mm gap." *User research* starts to look like *design,* doesn't it?[2]

I saw more blurring between research and design in another group that added a team member who was highly skilled at rapidly creating high-fidelity prototypes for developers. Research findings were delivered in exactly the right form that the internal customer needed.

Increase the visibility of your outputs. Look for as many possible audiences and venues to share your results. One of my clients took the deliverable we developed together and gave 30 presentations over a few months. Another team mounted an ever-growing number of user profile posters on the walls around their workspace (see Figure 9.6).

One researcher working on medical equipment did his prototyping at his desk instead of in a lab, and found that coworkers stopped by to investigate his progress. Another client of mine built a "museum" from our research in Japan that included miscellaneous consumer items and household equipment, pamphlets and advertisements, photographs, and printed pages from our research report. This display was in place for over a year and prompted conversations for years beyond that.

---

2   For an in-depth discussion of this dynamic, check out Andrew Harder's presentation "Critique, Don't Complain" at www.slideshare.net/andrewharder/critique-dont-complain-talk-by-andrew-harder and http://vimeo.com/19068092.

FIGURE 9.6
Field teams created profile posters, telling an engaging, visual story about an individual customer. The accumulated set of posters in the user research team's workspace raised awareness of that team's role.

Make sure that you have plenty of face time with the teams that will use your research. Spend some time each week in their location, if it's different than yours. Sit in on meetings, even if you aren't "invited." Share the user insights you already have that can inform their decisions and be on the lookout for opportunities to gather additional insights. The more you conduct deep and revealing interviews that drive the organization's thinking, the more impact you can have on almost everything in that organization. Good luck!

Summary

The emphasis here has been on gathering data in the field, but obviously we are doing that in order to do something with it: to unpack insights and turn them into opportunities for our teams to design new and better products and services. We also want to inform and inspire the organization with a richer and more nuanced perspective about the people we are serving.

- Working with research data is a combination of *analysis* (breaking larger pieces into smaller ones) and *synthesis* (combining multiple pieces into something new).

- From the experience you've had conducting the interviews, organize your initial takeaways into a topline report.

- Use the topline report to get early feedback from your team about what the research is starting to reveal. Uncover what insights may be challenging to accept and which ones are exciting. Use this intelligence to guide your deeper analysis.

- Divide up transcripts among team members. Review interviews and annotate transcripts to highlight insights, patterns, and quotes. Get the team back together and present interviews as case studies. Capture main points on sticky notes. Cluster stickies and write up your report.

- If your organization is resistant to interviewing users, identify the types of resistance you are facing, from cultural to resource (or other). Develop your response appropriately.

- Nothing sells like success. Leverage every bit of research you do to create opportunities for more research.

Index

discomfort
  identifying source, 121
  of interviewer, 123–125
  of participants, 78
disinterested interviewee, 22
distractions, avoiding, 19–20
documentation, 106–117
  audio recording, 108–109
  to clarify misinterpretations, 107
  debriefing, 115–117
  journaling by participants, 64
  note taking, 106–108
  photographs of interview, 112–113
  sketching, 113–114
  video recording, 112
"doorknob phenomenon," 80
DVD/digital projector, 61

E

effort silence, 89
emotion, 26
empathy, 10
environment for interviewing, 17
ethnography, 3. *See also* interviewing
exceptions, questions about, 90
expectations
  clear setting of, 120
  of client, 33
  questions about, 57
  social, 21
expertise of participant, 70
  respect for, 19
expert researchers, operating
    principles, 14
external market research recruiting
    agency, 37
eye contact, 25, 73
  while writing, 106

F

FaceTime, 126
facial expressions, coding system for, 26
failure silence, 89
feedback in recording, 26

field guide, 94
  creation, 39–43
  and interview process, 84
  participant background, 41
  use of, 69
field highlights, 117
field notes, 116
field team, roles for, 69–72
fieldwork
  participation guide, 69–70
  unstructured, 76–77
fight-or-flight reflex, 125
finding participants, 36–39
first impression, 22
flow, 95
focus group, 8
focus group companies, meeting
    rooms of, 127
follow-up questions, 86–87
framework, 14
Frank, Ted, 110–111

G

Gladwell, Malcolm, 26
goals, 17
  confirming with stakeholders, 31
GoToMeeting, 32
Gretzky, Wayne, 14
group dynamics, 128
groupings of interviews, 140
group therapy, 34–35

H

Hara, Kenya, 89
Harrell, Cyd, 32–33
Hausman, Todd, 96
Herzog, Werner, *Grizzly Man*, 85
Hewlett-Packard, 61
homework for participants, 63–65
humility, 19

I

images, for concept presentation, 62
improv show, 92
incentives, 46–48
  in releases, 45
information gathering, 3
insight
  in design process, 3–6
  vs. persuading organization, 2
intercept, 36
interpreting question, 87
interpretive notes, vs. descriptive, 108
interrupting participants, 122–123
interview guide, 39. *See also* field guide
interviewing
  adapting beginning, 75
  brief time for, 127
  ebb and flow, 94–95
  field guide and, 84
  flow management, 86–87
  getting more of answer, 87–89
  impact of, 10–11
  improving, 129–133
  limitations, 8
  in market research facility, 127
  by phone, 126–127
  of professionals vs. consumers, 127
  silence vs. awkwardness, 84–86
  technique of, 9–10
  variations and special cases, 125–129
  when to use, 7–9
interview stages, 69
  accepting awkwardness, 78
  crossing threshold, 72
  kick-off question, 78
  reflection and projection, 80
  restating objectives, 74–75
  soft close, 80
  tipping point, 79
iPods, transition between
    environments, 6

J

James, Caroline, 113, 114
Japan, silence in user research, 88–89
journaling, 64

K

kick-off question, 78
kinesthetic learning, 108
Kozinsky, Jerzy, *Being There*, 93
Kübler-Ross model of stages of grief, 68

L

language of participant, 96–97
leadership, research as activity, 141
lead interviewer, 70
lecture mode, avoiding, 102
lighting for video, 73, 110
listening, 24–27
  actively, 70
live recruiting, 33
LiveScribe smartpen, 108

M

mapping, 55–56
market research agencies, 39
  interview in facility, 127
market research, describing work as, 74
Maron, Marc, 100–101
McMullin, Jess, Design Maturity
    Model, 142
meltdown, 125
mental model of participant, 61
microphone
  external for audio recorder, 109
  placement, 110
Microsoft, 4
mind mapping, 113
mobile phone, silencing, 19
multiple participants, interviewing, 128

ACKNOWLEDGMENTS

The *ne plus ultra* of thanks is due to my family, for believing in the best of me and for their happiness for every bit of good stuff that comes my way. Such support is the *sine qua non* for my success. Thank you Anne, Sharna, Cheryl, Bruce, Talia, Ari, and Brody!

Going back decades, Tom Williams was there with me as we both began to "figger out" this whole user research thing. While we were initially focused on learning and doing, we eventually began teaching others (*discendo discimus!*), and many of my frameworks today emerged from that formative period. Even earlier, folks like Susan Wolfe and Marilyn Tremaine saw potential and pushed me to reach it.

For the genesis of this (and precursors), thanks are due to Deborah Rodgers, Dan Szuc, and Peter March. Ultimately, the biggest cheerleader for this project was Lou Rosenfeld, someone who transmutes *cacoethes scribendi* into fun and profit. During the writing, Lou's guidance and mentorship were invaluable, and my editor Marta Justak was a tireless and savvy source of advice, encouragement, compliments, and reassurance. Karen Corbett was there to make things happen when they needed to happen!

Right out of the gate, I found support from Elizabeth Goodman, Andrea Moed, Stefanie Norvaisas, and Marc Rettig, who happily agreed to serve as advisers, a role that neither they nor I fully grasped, and one I probably failed to sufficiently utilize. Still, *coniunctis viribus*!

David Hoard, Veronica Stuart, and Andrew Harder graciously served as technical reviewers. They read an early draft, and each contributed a colossal cornucopia of comments, calls for clarification, challenges, and compliments.

A whole heap of folks helped out with information, answers to questions, referrals, permission, content, or other succor. No doubt I'm forgetting quite a few (*mea culpa!*), but at least I know to thank Jennifer Ackerman, Kavita Appachu, Genevieve Bell, Jerry Birenz, Lena Blackstock, Harry Boadwee, Nate Bolt, Carla Borsoi, Al Bredenberg, Jan Chipchase, Tamara Christensen, Allan Chochinov, Elizabeth Churchill, Yohan Creemers, Anke de Jong, Arjen de Klerk, Richard Douglass, Donna Driscoll, Sheryl Ehrlich, Martin Elliott, Marc Fonteijn, Dave Franchino, Ted Frank, Leo Frishberg, Nancy Frishberg, Jorge Gordon, R. Reade Harpham, Cyd Harrell, Todd Hausman, Rachel Hinman, Eric Hixon, Miriam Home, Adrian Howard, Caroline James, Frances Karandy, Katie Koch, Jon Kolko, Livia Labate, Brenda Laurel, Douglas Look, Anna Lorenzetto, BJ Markel, Marc Maron, Christopher Mascis, Grant McCracken, Jess McMullin, Kirsten Medhurst, Adam Menter,

Lorri Meyers, Lindsey Miller, Steve Mulder, Michelle Nero, Julie Norvaisas, Nicolas Nova, Gary Paranzino, Julie Peggar, Michael Plishka, Jeff Pollard, Taciana Pontual, Cheryl Portigal-Todd, John Provost, Sarah A. Rice, Aviva Rosenstein, Kate Rutter, Dan Saffer, Liz Sanders, Lynn Shade, John Shortridge, Kristian Simsarian, Chad Singer, Carol Smith, Dan Soltzberg, Donna Spencer, Jared Spool, David St. John, Dörte Töllner, Mark Trammell, Timothy Tynyk, Dmitri von Klein, Jo Ann Wall, Pamela Walshe, Karen Ward, Russ Ward, Anne Williams, Tom Williams, Jeremy Yuille, Boris Zilberman, and Lindsey Zouein.

Finally, thanks to the hundreds of amazing, messy, complex, human people I've interviewed in the course of my career. I can only say *nemo nisi per amicitiam cognoscitur.*

Steve Portigal is the founder of Portigal Consulting, a bite-sized firm that helps clients to discover and act on new insights about themselves and their customers. Over the course of his career, he has interviewed hundreds of people, including families eating breakfast, hotel maintenance staff, architects, rock musicians, home-automation enthusiasts, credit-default swap traders, and radiologists. His work has informed the development of mobile devices, medical information systems, music gear, wine packaging, financial services, corporate intranets, videoconferencing systems, and iPod accessories.

Steve speaks regularly at corporate events and conferences such as CHI, IxDA, Lift, SXSW, UIE, UPA, UX Australia, UX Hong Kong, UX Lisbon, and WebVisions. His articles about culture, design, innovation, and interviewing users have been published in *interactions*, Core77, Ambidextrous, and Johnny Holland. He blogs at www.portigal.com/blog.

Steve built one of the first online communities (Undercover, a Rolling Stones fan group) in 1992, nurturing it from a time when the Internet was an underground academic technology through today.

After growing up near Toronto, Steve eventually made his way to the San Francisco Bay Area, where he's been for 20 years. He lives in the coastal town of Montara with his partner Anne and their furry dog Brody. Steve loves to travel, eat interesting food, and take pictures of travels and interesting foods and strange signs. He also really loves to nap.

You can reach Steve at www.portigal.com.